Religious Education in a
Secular Setting

J W D Smith

Religious Education in a Secular Setting

SCM PRESS LTD

177444

334 01393 3

First published 1969
by SCM Press Ltd
56 Bloomsbury Street London WC1

© SCM Press Ltd 1969

Printed in Great Britain by
Northumberland Press Limited
Gateshead

Contents

Acknowledgements

Grateful acknowledgements are made to the publishers for permission to quote from the following books and articles:

Associated Book Publishers Ltd: Melanie Klein, *Our Adult World and its Roots in Infancy*.

Basil Blackwell: M. Heidegger, *Being and Time* (Trans. John Macquarrie and Edward Robinson).

George Allen & Unwin Ltd: Bertrand Russell, *Autobiography of Bertrand Russell: 1914-1944*.
R. S. Peters, *Ethics and Education*.
A. Wedderspoon, ed., *Religious Education 1944-84*.

Hamish Hamilton Ltd: Bernard Berenson, *Sunset and Twilight*.

John Wilson (Farmington Trust Research Unit), *Aims of Education in Religion and the Emotions* (Working Paper circulated privately).

Oxford University Press: Ian T. Ramsey, *Models and Mystery*.

Penguin Books Ltd: John Wilson, Norman Williams and Barry Sugarman, *Introduction to Moral Education*.

Routledge and Kegan Paul Ltd: Edwin Cox, *Changing Aims in Religious Education*.
Simone Weil, *Gravity and Grace*.
Jean Piaget, *The Child's Conception of the World*.
Ludwig Wittgenstein, *Tractatus Logico-Philosophicus*.
Ronald Goldman, *Readiness for Religion*; *Religious Thinking from Childhood to Adolescence*.

The British Journal of Medical Psychology: Adah Maurer, 'Maturation of Concepts of Death' (Vol. 39, I, 1966).
Ernest Jones, 'The Psychology of Religion' (Vol. 6, 1926).

The Hogarth Press Ltd: Erik H. Erikson, *Childhood and Society*.

Yale University Press: Carl Gustav Jung, *Psychology and Religion*.

The extract from the series of work cards 'The Importance of Bread' by Margaret E. Hughes is reproduced by permission of Rupert Hart-Davies Educational Publications, London.

Preface

More than forty years ago I faced an audience of theological students as a deputy for their regular visiting lecturer in religious education. With the naïve confidence of youth I began by claiming that the practical problems of religious education raised basic questions about the nature of man, the nature of religion and the nature of the educational process. I was still an ignorant amateur in theology and I was uncomfortably aware of an amused, though friendly, gleam in the eyes of the more intelligent students. I knew that the amusement was justified but I was quite certain that I was directing their thoughts to questions that really mattered.

Retirement has brought leisure for reading and reflection at a time when the traditional religious foundations of education have been shaken, if not shattered, by scientific discovery and technical achievement. An invitation to lecture at the annual Scottish Conference on Christian Education at St Andrews provided an occasion for looking again at the old questions in a contemporary setting. I am grateful to the conference committee for the stimulus of this invitation. I am grateful also to the Student Christian Movement Press for encouraging me to revise the original lectures and to expand them considerably for publication.

Many books relevant to the general theme have been quoted, or mentioned, in the text. A selection of additional books of this type would be arbitrary and subjective and general bibliographies on religious education are readily available. For these reasons no bibliography has been provided.

Any merit which this book may have can be traced to the influence of others. Its errors and inadequacies are my own. My one hope is that it may encourage a new generation of teachers to look below the surface of current educational and theological controversies, to reflect more deeply on the meaning of religious education and to consider afresh its appropriate function in the schools and colleges of future years.

Jordanhill
March 1969

1   Clarifying our Aims

A timely and promising enterprise in the field of moral education began in Oxford in October 1965. A research unit was established under the auspices of the Farmington Trust. The Trust is administered by a Council under the chairmanship of A. D. C. Peterson, Director of the Department of Education at Oxford University. The research unit is the Trust's chief concern and it is expected that the work will continue for at least ten years. The first publication of the Research Unit was issued by Penguin Books Ltd in 1967 with the title *Introduction to Moral Education*.

The unit consists of a director and two research fellows. The director, John Wilson, read classics and philosophy at New College, Oxford, taught at King's School, Canterbury, spent a year as Professor of Religious Knowledge at Trinity College, Toronto, and then lectured in philosophy at Sussex University. One of the research fellows, Norman Williams, is a graduate in psychology and education from Durham University with twelve years' teaching experience, first in a secondary modern school and then in a school for maladjusted children. The third member of the team, Barry Sugarman, is a graduate in sociology from Exeter University, with five years' experience of post-graduate work in the U.S.A. and in London, which included study of the behaviour of teenagers at school.

The title of the unit's first publication is significant. One motive for the establishment of the unit, John Wilson tells us, 'was the feeling, now widely shared, that religious instruction alone could not provide a completely satisfactory framework for moral education'.[1] Two reasons are given in support of this view. The first is the diversity of belief and unbelief in contemporary society. The second is the lack of clarity among religious believers regarding the interpretation of their own beliefs and regarding the appropriate nature of religious education. This first publication attempts to clarify the nature of moral education and it includes substantial sections on the contributions of psychology and sociology.

Readers for whom moral and religious education are two aspects of one indivisible whole may find this book disappointing. Such readers may find themselves constrained, however, to re-examine their own presuppositions and to deepen their own thinking. The team itself may be compelled to dig more deeply into this aspect of their problem in later publications. A ten-year project can afford to begin in a leisurely fashion! The book exposes many fallacious arguments and prepares the ground systematically for future progress.

John Wilson has developed his own thoughts on religious education in a working paper on *Aims of Education in Religion and the Emotions* which was circulated privately in December 1967. His main concern in this paper was to stress the importance of clear and systematic thinking. He believes that the precise aim and intention of religious education has not been clearly stated because the nature of religion and its claim to a place in the educational curriculum have not been examined at sufficient depth. He supports his argument by quotations from Edwin Cox's *Changing Aims in Religious Education*. He commends the book for its general clarity and practical good sense but he finds it lacking in clarity of aim.

Edwin Cox names four possible aims in religious education. He rejects three as inadequate: teaching the Bible, teaching morals and converting to Christianity. He then states, in general terms, the aim which he considers acceptable in publicly maintained schools. It is 'to help pupils have a religious view of life and to make up their own minds on religious questions'.[2] He explains that

by religious view of life is meant these attitudes: that man is one part of the whole complex of creation, the most highly developed and sensitive part, but none the less bound in a close relationship with the other parts which are to be respected and not ruthlessly exploited for the pleasure either of the individual or the species; that the individual has to live among his fellows, who have to be accorded the same consideration that he gives himself; that the whole has some overall purpose which has to be sought, even if it can only be partially understood; that apprehension of that purpose will give a clue to practical decisions and lead to the adoption of a moral code; and that aesthetic experience, as well as rational thought, can give awareness of that purpose, so that natural beauty and the arts are to be revered and cultivated as one of the roads to truth.[3]

Cox acknowledges that these attitudes, or some of them, might figure in a general statement of educational aims and he defines the specifically religious features in his general statement:

What then is the specific aim of religious education? It will be to help cultivate these attitudes and, in particular, to help children to appreciate the questions that such attitudes raise, and consciously to seek the answers for themselves. These questions are of the type: 'Is creation adequately explained as a series of connected and mechanically caused events?'; 'Is there some spiritual reality of which the created world is but an outward manifestation?'; 'If so, does that spiritual reality reside in some single personal source which men have called "God"?'; 'Has an individual's life significance in its own right, or is it important only as part of some greater process?'; 'Is it possible for us to have any knowledge of what that significance is?'[4]

Wilson accepts much that is contained in Cox's statement of aim but he raises doubts about the specifically religious features in it. He writes:

Few rational people object to teaching children to respect and consider their fellows, or to appreciate natural beauty and the arts but plenty object to teaching children that 'the whole has an overall purpose' or that 'apprehension of that purpose will give a clue to practical decisions'. They would object to any mode of teaching which implied that children *ought* to ask, and try to answer . . . 'ultimate questions'. The objection is not to this or that specific 'religious answer' to 'religious questions' but to the whole business of persuading, or even helping, children to ask and answer questions of this sort: not to indoctrination in this or that particular religious view, but to indoctrination in the religious outlook generally.[5]

John Wilson is not stating his own views in these sentences. He is trying to diagnose the troubles of religious education in contemporary culture. He believes that writers like Edwin Cox, Harold Loukes, Ronald Goldman and 'many others' have not really penetrated to the heart of the contemporary problem. They have written 'very good books' on religious education but they have not clarified their aims. They have left themselves open to attack from opposite directions. Many non-Christian critics will accuse them of indoctrinating children in a religious outlook. Some Christian critics dislike their 'child-centred', 'open-ended' approach and would press for a more authoritarian presentation of Christian truth. Wilson admits the justice of the latter attitude. He says that the authors he has been criticizing

. . . do not offer us anything that might reasonably be called religious belief. What we are being offered is something that looks more like a political compromise than a genuine solution; and for that reason very remote, abstract, airy-fairy, and a long way from what the word 'religion' means to most ordinary people. . . . To talk of 'spiritual reality' or 'ultimate concern' may offend fewer people than talk about Jehovah and Jesus but it may also inspire fewer people.[6]

This array of lengthy quotations may seem tedious and unnecessary to many readers, but it certainly illustrates the need for clearer and deeper thinking about religious education. John Wilson's analysis of contemporary aims raises many questions which demand closer attention. It might be appropriate to begin with his assertion that 'plenty of people' would object to 'indoctrination in the religious outlook generally'. He is claiming that such people do not limit their objection to authoritarian teaching of particular doctrines. They object to any attempt to raise, and to discuss, religious questions with pupils in schools. Who are these people? How numerous are they? How much weight should be given to their objections?

It would be rash to offer an answer to such questions without the support of extensive and elaborate research. Such support is not available but a number of enquiries have been carried out in recent years which provide some relevant evidence. Parental attitudes to the religious provisions of the Education Act of 1944 were investigated by members of the Education Department of Newcastle University. Their findings were reported in *Learning for Living* in March 1967. They sent 3,232 questionnaires to representative groups of parents in the north-east of England, and 53·5% of them were returned. The questionnaires were supplemented by interviews with parents in the whole range of occupational groups and from varied age-groups. A substantial majority of these parents said that they were satisfied with the present compulsory provisions of the Act. The reasons given in support of religious education were revealing: 62% said that pupils should know about Christianity because Christianity is true; nearly 70% of all replies gave religious answers in favour of religious education. Two sentences from the parents of a twelve-year-old Newcastle child may be worth quoting: 'You have to have something to believe in in times of sorrow or if things go wrong. . . . Most of us are ordinary people, not brilliant or intellectuals.'[7]

There have been other similar enquiries. In 1963 Edwin Cox

made a limited study of attitudes to regular religious instruction among parents of sixth-form grammar-school pupils. He sent 2,278 questionnaires out and 76·5% of them were returned. Only 89 replies revealed opposition and almost 70% favoured regular religious instruction.[8] An article in *The New Society* in May 1965 showed 90% of the adult population in favour of the existing arrangements.

The general trend of opinion is sufficiently indicated by these surveys. On the basis of such evidence it could be claimed quite fairly that opposition to compulsory religious education in English schools – religious education with a Christian objective – would be confined to a minority of the population. The size of the minority would vary with the precise form of the question and with the circumstances in which it was put but it seems doubtful whether it would approach 50% in normal circumstances. Adult support for religious instruction on traditional lines is likely to be even stronger in Wales or Scotland. Does this mean that the current emphasis in books on religious education is unduly timid and apologetic? Should Christian teachers be leading a crusade in favour of authoritarian teaching of Christian beliefs and moral standards? Before the trumpets are sounded for such a crusade it would be wise to look more closely at two facts.

The first fact concerns the outlook and attitude of the parents whose views have been quoted. The Newcastle investigation of March 1967 raised questions about the religious commitment of those parents who completed their questionnaires. It would seem fair to assume that the 53·5% who returned the questionnaires had a genuine concern about the place of religious education in the schools. Of these parents 87% claimed affiliation with some religious denomination but only 25% claimed that they attended church regularly or fairly often.

This disconcerting glimpse is clarified and supplemented by a more extensive and elaborate survey of religious attitudes carried out in 1963-64 by the Gallup Poll organization. This survey showed 94% claiming membership of some religious denomination. Only 42% affirmed belief in a personal God. Less than a quarter said that they went to a place of worship as often as once a month and only 10% claimed that they had attended a service of worship on the preceding Sunday.

Such figures raise serious questions about the attitude of parents to religious education in the schools. Do parents who are so uncertain in their own convictions, and so wavering in their own religious loyalties, deserve to have their views on religious education taken seriously? Such a question is not easily answered. The reasons for perplexity in religious belief are obvious enough in our day. Motives for irregular church attendance are probably confused and irrational. The social habit of earlier generations has broken down and those who still attend church regularly may do so with greater personal conviction. But men and women who have lost all active connection with church life are still conscious, at times, of the uncertainties and insecurities of human existence. They include many 'ordinary people, not brilliant or intellectuals' who want 'something to believe in in times of sorrow or if things go wrong'. Parental concern may awaken this sense of need. Parents who show little outward sign of parental responsibility often retain a wistful hope that religious education may be good for their children. The remnants of religion in their own lives may be little more than ignorant prejudice and superstitious fear, but they know that there is something missing and they hope their children may find it.

It would be foolish to allow the feelings of such parents to influence the substance of religious education in the schools. Their views do not provide justification for evangelistic aims and authoritarian methods. It would be equally foolish to ignore the strength of their human concern. They know that their children need moral support and personal guidance which they have been unable to provide.

The second fact contains a powerful warning against any hasty acceptance of emotional pressure from parents. This fact becomes obvious when we look within the schools themselves. Here we find the children of those confused and inconsistent parents who support Christian teaching in the school but are vague and uncertain about their own beliefs and are thoroughly lax in their religious practices. These children are introduced at school to critical habits of thought. They are encouraged to seek empirical evidence and to rely on scientific types of proof. The mass media of communication exert an increasingly powerful influence on them. They are exposed to confused currents of religious belief and unbelief, to the uncontrolled expression of human emotion, to scenes of violence and suffering, to heroic human action and endurance by individuals, to the hollow promises of many politicians, to smooth words from many leaders of the establishment in church and state. Most of them pay little outward attention to it all, but they are growing to maturity in an atmosphere which makes them unresponsive to the voice of adult authority. Dogmatic religious teaching may offer a refuge to some at certain stages of their development but few can escape the persistent pressure of contemporary culture. Traditional religious language becomes meaningless. Christian values lose their traditional authority. Secondary-school pupils begin to experience the 'gulf' to which John A. T. Robinson referred in *Honest to God,* the 'gulf between the traditional orthodox supernaturalism in which our Faith has been framed and the categories which the "lay" world . . . finds meaningful today'.[9] Very few may be able to talk about this experience – even in the sixth form – but the experience leaves its mark on all secondary-school pupils. Few thoughtful teachers can doubt the existence of this gulf or be unaware of the problems it raises for religious education.

These problems affect the teacher as well as the pupil. The teacher in training is exposed to the empirical, anti-authoritarian mood of contemporary culture. Sociology plays an important part in college curricula. Linguistic analysis has a dominant place in the philosophy of education. Revealed truth is discarded and metaphysical thinking is out of fashion. It is becoming increasingly difficult for Christians and non-Christians to talk meaningfully with one another. During the twentieth century, Christian thinkers have been compelled to undergo a rigorous course of semantic discipline. Is 'God-language' viable in the world of universal human discourse or is it meaningful only within the private world of religious belief? Christian and non-Christian thinkers still wrestle with this question. The question is not answered, the debate goes on. Nevertheless much current writing on educational theory assumes that the matter is settled. 'God' is dead.

Students exposed to this atmosphere fall into several categories in their attitude to religious teaching. The majority of those preparing for secondary-school teaching feel themselves quite unfit to face the problems of religious teaching – even if they retain a residue of personal religious conviction. They are convinced that the subject must be taught by specialists. A minority are willing, and anxious, to undertake religious teaching and to prepare themselves for this additional responsibility. Some of that minority, and some of those who train as specialists, are unwilling to recognize the limitations of the class-room situation and to adapt themselves to it. They are evangelists rather than teachers and they carry the methods of the evangelist into the class room – with consequences which vary according to individual circumstances.

Nearly one hundred years have passed since the introduction of compulsory education in Britain. What is to happen to religious education in state maintained schools during the second century of compulsory education? John Wilson may have exaggerated the degree of opposition to religious education in the adult community. He was describing – and would know that he was describing – the attitude of a small sophisticated minority of intellectuals. But he is surely right in believing that the root of the difficulty and dissatisfaction within the schools lies in confusion of aim. Should religious education be recognized as an integral part of the educational curriculum? Would that imply full acceptance of the 'pupil-centred', 'open-ended' approach? Would it mean adopting an objective sociological-historical approach to religious beliefs and institutions at the secondary-school level? What *would* it mean? Should we aim, on the other hand, at a more full-blooded Christian approach by fully committed teachers within the normal school time-table and under the existing statutory provisions? Should we openly profess the evangelistic aim which most critics expect and which many parents seem to want? What would be the fruits of such a policy within the schools? The mere framing of such questions underlines John Wilson's contention. We cannot begin to answer them without giving serious thought to the nature of religion and to its place in the normal development of human personality.

2 The Historical Background

Universal popular education under state control began in Britain about a hundred years ago. The nineteenth-century movement towards that goal was socially conditioned. Industrial development had created new social needs and awakened new social demands. The immediate educational objectives were limited. Popular education was primarily concerned with the basic knowledge and skills needed for intelligent citizenship. Personal development was still regarded as the responsibility of the home and the church.

The place of religion in a national system of education was a thorny problem. Scottish circumstances differed from those in England and Wales but the administrative solution was similar. The state adopted a neutral attitude. No government grant was made available for religious purposes. Religious activities were not subject to government inspection. A conscience clause permitted parents to withdraw their children from periods of religious worship and teaching. The initiative in religious matters was left to the local administrative unit.

Popular education in England and Wales before the Education Act of 1870 had been dependent on religious and philanthropic initiative. Government grants and government supervision had increased steadily from 1833 but the schools were owned and managed by churches and other voluntary bodies. Denominational differences were acute and religion was a storm centre of educational debate. The neutrality of the state was safeguarded in the Act by the Cowper-Temple clause which forbade the use of any 'religious catechism or religious formulary distinctive of any particular denomination' in schools which received financial support from local rates.

The growth of board schools in England and Wales was comparatively slow at first. In the closing years of the nineteenth century they were only two-fifths of the total, and accommodation in church schools alone was still considerably greater than in board schools. Denominational rivalry remained strong but the Cowper-Temple clause safeguarded denominational interests in the board schools. The state acknowledged that the home and the churches were primarily responsible for transmission of the tribal mores. The board schools had a humbler, utilitarian objective.

The situation changed rapidly during the early decades of the twentieth century. The objectives of popular education were steadily enlarged. The development of individual potentiality began to claim a place alongside earlier social and vocational aims. Educational costs mounted steeply. Denominational resources were severely strained and increased state grants were accompanied by limitation of denominational control. Denominational rivalry gradually gave way to co-operation. The public sector of education had become so large and so important that religious education in the council and county secondary schools became a topic of increasing concern. The churches took counsel with one another and the preparation of 'agreed syllabuses' began. *The Cambridgeshire Syllabus of Religious Teaching for Schools* (1924) was an important landmark in this movement. It was prepared by an 'Advisory Committee consisting of members of the Church of England, the Free Churches, and of teachers in various kinds of schools and training colleges. It was expressly designed to be an *agreed* Syllabus with the two-fold object of ensuring . . . that religious teaching and observance in all types of school administered by the Education Committee should be adequate and based on sound foundations.'[1]

Interdenominational co-operation increased steadily in range and in depth. An international conference on *Church, Community and State* was held at Oxford in July 1937. Christian leaders came together from many lands, and many denominations, to consider the responsibilities and tasks of Christian churches in the contemporary world. Education was one of the themes considered in a series of preparatory volumes issued in connection with the conference. The outbreak of the Second World War added urgency to Christian thought and action. Many thoughtful people, outside as well as within the churches, were troubled by the lack of clear social purpose and conviction in the country. Plans were being made for extensive educational development and new thought was given to the place of religion in these plans.

The outlook of the period is clearly indicated in the *White Paper on Educational Reconstruction* of 1943. The section on religious education contained the following sentence: 'There has been a very general wish, not confined to representatives of the Churches, that religious education should be given a more defined place in the life and work of the schools, springing from the desire to revive the spiritual and personal values in our society and in our national tradition.' Many years of denominational co-operation were about to bear remarkable fruit in a period of national concern. The state was about to accept a new educational responsibility.

The Education Act of 1944 made religious worship and teaching compulsory, throughout England and Wales, in all schools maintained by a local education authority. The Act retained the form of the Cowper-Temple clause but altered its impact. The clause now stated that religious worship 'shall not be distinctive of any particular religious denomination' and that religious teaching should be given 'in accordance with an agreed syllabus . . . [which] shall not include any catechism or formulary which is distinctive of any particular denomination'.[2] The fifth schedule of the Act made it obligatory for all local education authorities to prepare an agreed syllabus or adopt an existing one. Such a syllabus was to be produced by a conference consisting of four committees representing respectively the local authority, the Church of England, other religious denominations and the teachers. The Act still rejected denominational worship and teaching but the provisions for syllabus preparation ensured that the substance and intention of religious education would be Christian. The state assumed direct responsibility for moral and religious education on a Christian basis.

The Education (Scotland) Act of 1872 also safeguarded the neutrality of the state in religious matters but there was a significant difference. The Act brought a variety of existing agencies under state direction and provided for further expansion. Parish schools, provided by local landowners and superintended by the local parish minister, had existed under statutes dating back to 1646. Deficiencies in the parish school system had been partially overcome by religious and charitable initiative. Religious traditions were predominantly Presbyterian and these traditions had been fostered as diligently in the statutory parish schools as in the schools provided and managed by denominational bodies. Denominational differences were less acute than in England and Wales but religious controversy prevented

the perpetuation of religious worship and teaching under direct
state control.

The initiative was passed to the local school boards, as in England,
but no corresponding restriction was placed on the substance of
the teaching. There was no 'Cowper-Temple clause'. The school
boards were empowered to continue religious worship and teaching
'in accordance with use and wont'. They did so and religious teaching continued to be based on the Bible and the Shorter Catechism.
The state remained neutral but local decision fostered the traditional
Presbyterian mores.

The influence of the church remained strong for many years.
Ministers played a leading part in the early school boards and the
traditional parish school practice of ministerial inspection of
religious teaching lingered for many years. It was eventually superseded by the appointment of ministers as honorary school chaplains
in many educational areas. These chaplains are recognized as
honorary members of the school staff and are available to advise
and assist in religious activities at the discretion of the head teacher.
Co-operation between representatives of the non-Roman churches
and various educational interests has been fostered by a joint committee which has issued syllabuses and other teachers' aids for
school use. The training of non-Roman Catholic teachers came
under public control but provision was made for church control of
religious education in these colleges. In 1946 this responsibility was
transferred to the governing body acting under the Scottish Education Department.

The statutory position of religious worship and teaching in the
schools has remained essentially unchanged from 1872 to the present
time. Responsibility still rests upon the local education authority.
No authority may discontinue the traditional practice without
securing approval from the local electorate but the substance and
the quality of the teaching has been affected by social and cultural
changes. Aim, content and methods vary in different areas and in
individual schools. Many local education authorities now employ
specially qualified teachers in secondary schools but their status is
uncertain and their prospects of promotion are slender. In some
schools religious education reaches a high standard. In others the
traditional practice is represented now by little more than a time-
table entry.

The position of religious education has come under critical

scrutiny throughout Britain during the last ten years or so. A series of English enquiries into the effects of the 1944 Act produced disconcerting results. A representative conference promoted by the London University Institute of Education surveyed the situation and re-examined the place of religion in education. The response of pupils in secondary schools to the teaching which they received was described by Harold Loukes of the Oxford University Department of Education. He summarized impressions derived from personal investigations in these devastating words:

If we look back at the story thus far, we are left with a dismal picture of failure. We try for ten years to teach the 'facts' of the Bible, and we fail. We encourage our pupils to read it for themselves, and they refuse. We try to convey, through the biblical narratives, the development of the idea of God, and we fail. We gather our pupils together for a total of 2,000 daily acts of worship, and we leave the vast majority indifferent, hostile, or bitterly resentful. Within the year, they will have cut themselves off entirely from Bible, Christian imagery and Christian practice, and will take nothing with them except muddled memories of life in a child-sized church.[3]

The Act of 1944 had not fulfilled the hopes of those who planned the religious sections. What had gone wrong? Ronald Goldman's *Religious Thinking from Childhood to Adolescence* (London: Routledge and Kegan Paul, 1964) had provided solid evidence in support of those who distrusted the traditional Bible-centred syllabus. On the basis of personal research he claimed that religious teaching had failed because it had tried to do 'too much too soon'. Harold Loukes's own book *Teenage Religion* (London: SCM Press, 1961) and his later one *New Ground in Christian Education* (London: SCM Press, 1965) had focused attention on the importance of relating religious teaching to the real interests and needs of the pupils. *An Open Letter to L.E.A. Religious Advisory Committees* was prepared and circulated in 1965 by a group of university and college lecturers who shared a common concern for the unhappy state of religious education. They stated that they were 'particularly concerned with the way in which the subject as taught in schools has lost touch with the situation outside. It is presented as if the society in which we live were fully Christian and the pupils all came from Christian homes.'

An Anglican Commission on Religious Education in Schools began work under the chairmanship of the Bishop of Durham in 1967. It expects to issue its findings in 1969. The British Council of Churches initiated a thorough enquiry into the position of religious education in the county secondary schools of England and Wales, which was financed by the Gulbenkian Foundation and carried out by Colin Alves, now of Brighton College of Education. The report was published under the title *Religious Education and the Secondary School* (London: SCM Press, 1968). It is thorough, realistic and forward looking and it makes an important contribution to Christian thinking. Such reports suffer from one serious weakness. They are prepared by Christians and they are addressed primarily to Christians. They tend therefore to make Christian assumptions which limit their appeal to non-Christians. State policy is still responsive to intelligent and informed Christian opinion but this may prove to be a wasting asset. It may be time for Christian educators to think and to speak primarily as educators. In the long run religion can only retain a secure place in the curriculum of state schools if it can be shown to make an essential contribution to personal development in childhood and adolescence.

Scottish opinion has crystallized more slowly but dissatisfaction with the position of religious education in Scottish schools has been expressed more openly and more strongly in recent years. Representations have been made to the Scottish Education Department by representative church and educational bodies, and the Secretary of State for Scotland set up a committee to review moral and religious education in Scottish schools (other than Roman Catholic schools) in July 1968. The committee includes humanists as well as Christians but it has been instructed to work within the limits of the existing statutory framework. The 'use and wont' tradition is still sacrosanct.

The state has steadily accepted more and more of the responsibilities which used to be left to the home and to the churches. A much richer, and more varied, curriculum has been developed to supplement the limitation of the home environment. Extra-mural activities and various forms of school 'counselling' now enrich the normal pastoral relationship of teachers with their pupils. The state school has moved steadily in this direction under the pressure of social need but its plans have not been guided by a clear philosophy.

Compulsory religious education, with a Christian intention, was introduced in England and Wales in the belief that public opinion favoured an educational system which would 'educate for democracy based on Christian principles' (leading article in *The Times* of July

17, 1944). This change in policy was already anachronistic. It was made at a time of national stress and emotional unity, but post-war developments soon revealed a widening gap between traditional Christianity and the opinions and attitudes of modern society. No corresponding change was made in Scotland but there, too, emotion tends to confuse the real issues. The religious tradition in Scottish schools still depends on local sentiment and initiative, but few are willing to acknowledge openly the insecurity and uncertainty of such a foundation. The fiction still persists among Christians on both sides of the border that church and school are partners in a common enterprise of Christian education. That fiction is now wearing very thin.

Educational policy in state maintained schools has reached the frontiers of religion. It has already crossed these frontiers in England and Wales but the path it chose to follow now looks unpromising. Future policy in Scotland is still uncertain. Those responsible for educational policy in both parts of the country are well aware of the state's responsibilities for moral, if not religious, education. How can the state fulfil these responsibilities appropriately in a society which is confused and divided in religious belief and in moral practice?

Christians have been talking with one another about future policy. Realistic Christian assessments of the situation have been made. Important recommendations on policy have been brought forward. The debate between Christians still goes on – and must go on. But the debate between educators, Christian and non-Christian, has hardly begun. Educators no longer use traditional religious language. They are not concerned, as educators, with traditional religious language, but they cannot ignore the problems to which traditional religious education was originally addressed. An attempt must be made to explore these problems in the common language which Christian educators share with their non-Christian colleagues. The nature of religion and its place in personal development must be examined at greater depth. The relationship between morality and religion must be explored. The point at which Christian and non-Christian educators are compelled to part company in their thinking must be clearly exposed. We must ask whether Christians and non-Christians could co-operate in a common policy for religious and moral education in state schools. We must begin to consider what type of curriculum might be acceptable.

3 Can We Still Use Religious Language?

The metaphysical problem 'Does God exist?' has been replaced by the linguistic question 'Is the word "God" meaningful?' This latter question has moved to the centre of contemporary thinking about religion. Is religious language still meaningful universally or is it now a private language which is only meaningful within the limited world of religious belief? This question has an obvious bearing on the future of religious education in state schools. If religious language is no longer meaningful to everybody it would surely follow that religious education would only be viable within the limited circle of religious believers.

Ludwig Wittgenstein was one of the most important figures in the movement of philosophical interest from metaphysics to linguistics. He was born in Austria and trained as an engineer. His studies took him to Manchester where he became interested in the logical foundations of mathematics. He developed this interest at Cambridge under Bertrand Russell before the First World War. He served as an officer in the Austrian army during the war and wrote his first book while on combatant service in Italy.

Bertrand Russell included extracts from some of Wittgenstein's letters in *The Autobiography of Bertrand Russell: 1914-1944*. Some of these letters were written in English and they are reproduced without alteration of spelling or syntax. One such letter, written from Cassino on August 19, 1919, provides valuable insight into the central argument of Wittgenstein's book. '. . . Now I'm affraid you haven't realy got hold of my main contention, to which the whole business of logical props is only a corolary. The main point is the theory of what can be expressed (*gesagt*) by props – i.e. by linguage – (and, which cames to the same, what can be *thought*) and what can not be expressed by props, but only shown (*gezeigt*); which, I believe, is the cardinal problem of philosophy.'[1]

Russell's failure to recognize immediately Wittgenstein's 'main contention' is not altogether surprising. The book as a whole is devoted to a close logical analysis of the nature and use of propositions ('props'). It has the daunting title *Tractatus Logico-Philosophicus*. The preface is dated Vienna 1918. In the preface he claims that metaphysical problems – such as the problems of God, Freedom and Immortality which concerned Immanuel Kant and a long succession of philosophical writers – are not *real* problems. They arise, he says, from confusion in our use of language. He attempts, therefore, to formulate the conditions for a logically perfect language.

Wittgenstein's book is almost as daunting as its title but its argument, as far as it need concern us here, can be summed up in a few brief quotations. In the preface he tells us that 'the whole meaning [of the book] . . . could be summed up somewhat as follows: what can be said at all can be said clearly: and whereof one cannot speak thereof one must be silent'. He goes on to assert that all meaningful propositions are those of the natural sciences. We can only speak clearly and meaningfully about empirical knowledge. Philosophy can add nothing to human knowledge.

Towards the close of his book Wittgenstein makes several assertions which illustrate the 'main contention' to which he referred in his letter to Russell. 'We feel,' he writes, 'that even if *all possible* scientific questions be answered, the problems of life have still not been touched on at all. Of course there is then no question left, and just this is the answer. The solution of the problem of life is seen in the vanishing of this problem.'[2] The problem, in Wittgenstein's view, is an unreal problem which only arises because we have failed to recognize the limits of logical language. He does, however, add a significant but cryptic admission: 'there is indeed the inexpressible. This shows itself: it is the mystical.'[3]

'The cardinal problem of philosophy', according to Wittgenstein, was to distinguish clearly between those matters which could be expressed in logical propositions and those which could only be 'shown'. His book closes with a repetition of the words quoted from his preface: '*Wovon man nicht sprechen kann, darüber muss man schweigen.*' These words might be freely rendered as follows: 'We must be silent about those matters which we cannot talk about meaningfully.' If we accept Wittgenstein's contention we seem to be driven to the conclusion that 'God-language' is not universally meaningful. Its subject-matter belongs to that which may be 'shown' but cannot be expressed in logical propositions. 'God-language' belongs to the private world of religious belief.

Wittgenstein modified his position considerably in later years. His second book has a preface dated from Cambridge in 1945. By that time he had become a very influential figure in English philosophy. The book was first published in English with the title *Philosophical Investigations* in 1953, two years after his death. The most notable feature in this book, from our standpoint, is its admission that human language is used quite legitimately in many different ways. There is no one ideal logical structure which governs the meaningful use of language in all circumstances. Recognition of this fact leads him to introduce the concept of the 'language-game'. A game has rules which have a limited application. So also there are appropriate rules which should govern the use of language in different areas of human discourse. We cannot take the rules which govern the use of language in the discussion of empirical facts and expect that these same rules will apply universally. He writes: 'Am I less certain that this man is in pain than that twice two is four? . . . The kind of certainty is the kind of language-game.'[4]

This is certainly an important change of position. Wittgenstein is now acknowledging that human language may be used meaningfully in many different ways. Confusion in the use of language arises from the fact that 'the clothing of our language makes everything alike'. This common 'clothing' hides logical differences in the use of language. Wittgenstein does not relate this general principle to the particular case of religious language but the implications are clear enough. The statement 'God exists' has not the same meaning as the statement 'The sun exists'. The two propositions wear the same clothing but they are not governed by the same logical rules. They belong to two different 'language-games'.

Many contemporary theologians and philosophers have wrestled with the problem of religious language. They have tried to analyse the logical structure and status of religious assertions. Ian T. Ramsey and other Christian theologians believe that theology can profit greatly from the contemporary philosophical interest in language. It 'can be so developed as to provide a novel inroad into the problems and controversies of theology, illuminating its claims and reforming its apologetics'.[5] In his later book, *Models and Mystery*, he shows very clearly that critical analysis of the nature and use of religious language may help to build bridges between theology and other areas of human thought and experience. The lectures published with this title were planned and delivered as an essay in inter-faculty bridge-building. The subjects of university study are becoming so specialized that meaningful communication between specialists in different fields is becoming almost impossible. Ramsey's lectures were planned as a bridge building enterprise at a particularly difficult point.

The essence of Ramsey's argument lies in his conviction that the use of conceptual models and the acknowledgment of ultimate mystery are characteristic features in modern science and in theology. He begins by distinguishing between picturing models, or scale models, and disclosure or analogue models. He uses a quotation from Lord Kelvin to illustrate the meaning of a picturing or scale model. Kelvin's *sine qua non* for understanding any problem of physics was a mechanical model. ' "I never satisfy myself," he said, "until I can make a mechanical model of a thing. If I can make a mechanical model, I can understand it. Unless I can make a mechanical model all the way through, I cannot understand it." '[6]

These words remind us of the weird but intriguing mechanical models of the solar system which used to be commonplace objects in museums. They were not scale models in the strict sense of the term. A scale model of the solar system in which the sun, the earth with its moon, and the other planets with their satellites were all of visible size and in scaled proportion could obviously not be housed in a museum. Several scales were employed and such models gave a very helpful, though very misleading, impression which helped to interpret the theoretical knowledge which could be derived from books. Although it was not strictly a scale model, it was, in Ramsey's phrase, a useful 'picturing model'.

Ramsey reminds us that the era of 'picturing models' belongs now to the history of science. Modern physics or astronomy, and other branches of modern science, use conceptual models. The aim of the picturing model was to imitate the original as far as circumstances permitted. The aim of the conceptual model is to reproduce the *structure*, 'the web of relationships' (a phrase quoted by Ramsey from a book by Max Black) with which scientific research is concerned. The astronomer may employ such a model to assist him in solving some problem in outer space. Certain phenomena are observed by optical or radio telescopes which do not fit into any known pattern of theoretical explanation. The theoretical astronomer seeks a convenient conceptual model which will express the web of relationships between the physical forces operating, or believed to be operating, at that point in space. This model echoes the structure of the physical phenomena in a simplified form which permits mathematical expression and mathematical treatment. The mathematical possibilities of the situation are worked out by use of the model. Explanatory hypotheses then emerge which can be verified, or rejected, by observational methods. Ramsey emphasizes the distinction between this type of model and the picturing model of Kelvin's day. The modern type of model does not provide a picture of the universe. There are analogies between the structure of the model and the empirical phenomena, but the models are not minia-ture descriptive pictures. They are convenient tools for extending scientific understanding.

Ramsey calls such models *disclosure* models. He points out that such a model is conceived in a moment of insight which is also a moment of disclosure. No useful model can be framed in intellectual detachment from the empirical phenomena. The model emerges in the mind of the scientist who is continually concerned with these phenomena. In Ramsey's words: 'The universe itself authenticates a model. The model arises in a moment of insight when the universe discloses itself in the points where the phenomena and the model meet. In this sense there must be at the heart of every model a "disclosure".'[7]

Ramsey gives other illustrations drawn from the fields of psycho-logy and sociology. The rat provides a simplified, more easily observed, model of human behaviour. Surgical experiments may be carried out on rats which could not be used on human beings. Deductions from such experiments may be used to interpret human behaviour. The machine that plays chess may be a useful simplified model for the interpretation of human thinking. Probability theory may be used in psychological and sociological research to interpret facts about human intelligence and social behaviour. In all such cases the scientists concerned are using models of the *disclosure* type. Such models cannot give a descriptive account of the human mind or of human behaviour. They are not picturing models of the Kelvin type. They are aids to scientific understanding.

Ramsey draws attention to the logical limits which are reached when such models are used in psychology or sociology. The study of human nature, human thinking and human behaviour necessarily treats man as an object but the observer who carries out the investigation is also a participant in the activities he describes. Human subjectivity imposes a logical limit on the intellectual understanding which such models can provide. Fuller understanding of human nature requires insights of a different order. These insights may be expressed in language but the language has a different logical structure and status. In the human sciences the experimenter meets mystery which the model does not dispel.

In other words let us not blind our eyes to the logical discrepancy between the mathematical models which in the most democratic fashion unite us profitably with the rats, and the insights for which the sort of language used by Shakespeare may well be more reliable currency. Here is an insight into ourselves to which no models however illuminating will ever be completely adequate . . . Here is the meeting place *par excellence* of models and mystery: in what to each of us is the disclosure of himself.[8]

Ramsey argues that theology also uses a type of disclosure model. His argument here needs to be supplemented by the fuller discussion which the topic receives in his earlier book *Religious Language*. There he shows how the special features of religious language arise from the nature of religious situations. These situations always involve disclosure, insight or discernment and also total commitment. The combination of disclosure and commitment is characteristic of every religious conversion. It is also characteristic of every moment of real growth in Christian experience. Christian preaching, or teaching, may fall on deaf ears, as we say, ninety-nine times out of a hundred. Then one day, for reasons which defy analysis, 'the penny drops', as Ramsey puts it, and a flash of insight transforms a human life. The situation involves disclosure, discernment and commitment.

When the theologian tries to talk about such religious experiences he also uses models. They are not constructed in intellectual detachment, they arise or are verified in some moment of experience. Some historical, temporal events acquire a significance which transcends space and time. The familiar hymn of the Merchant Navy 'Eternal Father strong to save' might become a vehicle of disclosure, discernment and commitment to a merchant seaman in a situation of extreme danger. He might have sung that hymn many times but this time 'the penny dropped'. The universe disclosed itself to him in the metaphor of a father's love and power to help. In such a situation fatherhood is confirmed as a model through which the universe is disclosed. The model is not of the Kelvin type. It is not a picturing model. It does not describe a super-human being in outer space who can be trusted to bring the ship safely to land. It is a disclosure model. It helps to articulate the insight and disclosure experience in a significant human situation.

The word *eternal* acts as a very important qualifier of the model. The presence of such qualifying words is, says Ramsey, a *sine qua non* of all religious language. It makes clear the fact that the noun points beyond itself to the permanent mystery which lies at the heart of theology. The word *God* is the key-word of religious language. It expresses 'the kind of commitment' which the religious man professes. Religious language seeks to interpret this word by countless metaphors and models drawn from the world of space and time but all religious words have some qualifying term like *first* cause, *infinitely* wise, *perfect* love, *eternal* father and so on. Such qualifying words remind us of the limits of language. The models and metaphors of religion may be drawn from the world of space and time but they do not offer descriptive pictures of the cosmos. They are not picturing models. They are disclosure models which offer insight into the nature of God and which invite total commitment to God.

It is quite impossible, in a few paragraphs, to do justice to Ian Ramsey's brilliant application of linguistic analysis to theology. Here is a brave attempt to turn an apparent enemy of religious belief into a friend and ally. Ramsey uses the methods of linguistic analysis to show that religious language has its own inner logic appropriate to the nature of its subject-matter. Theology is a 'language-game', in Wittgenstein's phrase, with its own rules, its own insights and its own acknowledgment of ultimate mystery. All intellectual disciplines use models or metaphors. All find insight through such models. Ramsey claims that theology, in fellowship with other intellectual disciplines, can contribute to a fuller understanding of the mystery to which – in common with all such disciplines – it can only point.

Has Ramsey provided us with an answer to our question? Can religious language be used meaningfully outside the limits of the believing community? A negative answer is inevitable. His book is a brave attempt at bridge-building between theologians and other university specialists. Critical analysis of religious language is a valuable and astringent discipline for contemporary theology. It may help to re-establish its intellectual respectability in the eyes of some critics. It does not, and cannot, restore traditional religious language to universal currency.

The disclosure models of theology are subject to a serious limitation. In Ramsey's argument they seem, by analogy, to offer a means of advancing human understanding as conceptual models do in the physical sciences, but Ramsey has to admit that they differ in a significant way from the models of the scientist. The theologian has no objective means of verifying the increased understanding which his models seem to offer. The insights which mathematical models yield in astronomical research can be tested by empirical observation. The disclosure model 'Eternal Father' cannot be tested in the same objective way.

Ramsey claims that the models of religious language are judged by 'the method of empirical fit'. A shoe may fit, or not fit, the foot of a pedestrian. It may seem to fit when he tries it on in a shop but the real test comes when the shoe is in daily use. The insights offered by the disclosure models of the theologian are tested on the highway of life. The argument is attractive. It is entirely satisfactory within its own limits but it ends inevitably in a subjective judgment. The shoe which fits one man may not fit another. Religious language may interpret the experience of some but be meaningless to others. The models and metaphors of religious language cannot deepen religious insight in those who have made no religious commitment. They convey as little meaning to the uncommitted as descriptions of a sunset do to the colour blind.

The word mystery also deserves closer examination. It may be used in more than one way. The empirical scientist uses the tools of his science to dispel the false mysteries arising from human ignorance and superstition. He tries to push back the frontiers of human knowledge. But empirical scientists may find that the very nature of human existence imposes a limit on further understanding. The astronomer knows that the theory of the expanding universe carries an inevitable corollary. According to this theory galaxies are receding at a speed which increases as their distance increases. It follows that a distance must inevitably be reached at which their speed of recession seems to exceed the speed of light. Light from such galaxies can never reach us. The astronomer has reached the limits of the observable universe. As a human being he may be stirred by a sense of mystery. He will not attempt to penetrate *that* mystery by the methods of science. Like the old Negro preacher he does not 'pretend to know the unknowable or to unscrew the inscrutable, (he) just co-operates with the inevitable'. As an astronomer he uses the tools of his science to dispel all false mystery. As a human being he may be stirred by the true mystery which has its source in the very nature of human existence. In Wittgenstein's terminology this is 'the mystical' which 'shows itself'.

Ramsey issues a useful warning to the social scientists. He reminds them that there is a logical limit to their use of models. This limit arises from the nature of their subject-matter. In the social sciences man is both observer and observed and there are aspects of man's nature, as observer, which elude detached scientific observation. Man the observer is a centre of personal thought and feeling whose inner nature cannot be laid bare by statistical studies or simplified models. These methods may dispel the mystery which arises from human ignorance. They cannot interpret the complexities of personal existence. The insight of the poet may penetrate to depths which experimental psychology and sociology cannot reach. Here, too, we are in the region of 'the mystical' where truth 'shows itself'.

There is no true parallel between the conceptual models of the scientist and the disclosure models of the theologian. The former may dispel the clouds of mystery which arise from human ignorance and superstition. The latter offer ways of speaking meaningfully about religious insights into the true mystery at the core of human existence. But such insights are not universally valid. Their truth cannot be verified by objective tests. Theology may be a meaningful 'language-game' in Wittgenstein's sense. It may have its own inherent logical structure. It may be a thoroughly respectable intellectual discipline. But it is not a game which everyone would be willing to play.

Psychologists use a different language-game to describe, and interpret, the phenomena of religious experience. The conversion of a merchant seaman can be described, and interpreted, in psychological or in religious language. Some psychologists are Christians. They are bi-lingual. They would be able, in different contexts, to describe a conversion experience in psychological and in religious terminology. They would freely acknowledge, however, that the religious description was based on assumptions which, as psychologists, they were unable to make. Religious insight belongs to that region in which truth 'shows itself'. Religious language cannot be truly meaningful without religious commitment. Traditional religious language has become a private language in the modern world because traditional religious commitment is a minority experience. This is the basic problem of religious education today.

The problem is not confined to state schools. Teachers in denominational schools and in church organizations do not escape from it. They meet it in the earlier years of childhood and in adolescence. The symbolical nature of religious language raises difficulties with younger children in all circumstances. Consider the opening words of a familiar nineteenth-century hymn:

> Above the clear blue sky,
> In heaven's bright abode.

Young children naturally interpret such words literally and materially. Can traditional religious language be used in the primary school without distorting children's thinking and clouding their religious insight? This whole subject requires separate discussion but one important point may be noticed in passing. The symbolical nature of religious language is likely to raise fewer difficulties for pupils who are in living contact with Christian belief and practice at home and in church. Religious language is associated, for them, with experiences at the level of feeling and attitude which contain the seeds of spiritual growth. It is easier for such pupils to pass from a material to a spiritual interpretation of religious symbolism. They may reject the language of the hymn as childish and inadequate but they will not necessarily reject the symbol 'Heavenly Father' when they cease to believe in a material and spatial heaven.

The problem of religious language is no new one for teachers of young children but the decay of religious belief makes it more acute. In the primary classes of state schools there are increasing numbers of children for whom religious language is little more than an intellectual puzzle. It has no meaningful associations in their everyday experience. Such children illustrate most clearly the problem of religious education in a secular setting. Teachers in denominational schools and in church organizations do not escape the problem but they meet it in a different form. Religious language may be more familiar to their pupils but it may be almost equally meaningless. Familiarity with religious language makes the educational problem even more difficult if the language is associated with purely formal and conventional belief and practice. This kind of familiarity is common enough in state schools also.

The problem of religious language takes a different form in adolescence. The secularizing influences of modern culture penetrate every class room and every home. The influence of traditional religion may be stronger in denominational schools and in the homes of some state-school pupils but the strength of that influence merely changes the character of the problem. A growing number of adolescent boys and girls in state schools find religious language quite meaningless and irrelevant. They think and speak in the scientific, secular idiom of contemporary humanism or materialism. Such pupils present the religious educator with a peculiarly difficult task of communication. They illustrate the magnitude of the problem which religious education must face in a secularized society.

The situation in denominational schools and in church organizations is different. The state-school situation, too, is far from uniform. The cultural time lag leaves areas and social groups in which the authority of traditional belief and life is still strong. Adolescent boys and girls in these settings are faced with a conflict between two languages which seem mutually incompatible. Traditional religious words like God, providence, creation, grace, sin and forgiveness cannot be translated easily into the language of contemporary culture. Some boys and girls will cling to the security of tradition in their own personal lives and adopt secular language as the vehicle of vocational and social communication. A very few will struggle to integrate the two ways of thinking. At the adolescent stage many will be troubled by emotional conflict and torn between acceptance and rejection of religious tradition. The nature and intensity of the struggle will depend, in part, on the reality and power of religious influences in earlier years. It will take different forms according to the temperament and intelligence of individual pupils. The problem of traditional religious language lies at the heart of religious education in every type of school. It is not possible, any longer, to isolate children from 'the acids of modernity'.

4   Is Moral Education Enough?

John Wilson tells us that one motive for establishing the Farmington Trust research unit on moral education was 'the feeling, now
widely shared, that religious education alone could not provide a
completely satisfactory framework for moral education'.[1] He men-
tions two reasons for this 'widespread feeling'. The first is the
plurality of religious belief and unbelief in contemporary society.
The second is the confusion among religious leaders regarding the
interpretation of their own belief and regarding the appropriate
substance and methods of religious education.

Both reasons are valid and weighty. A deep concern for more
effective moral education unites many who are sharply divided in
matters of religious belief. Why should we not concentrate on moral
education in state schools and ensure a full measure of co-operation
from teachers of many different religious opinions? Is religious
education not essentially a confessional concern? Should it not be
left to the churches and planned by them in accordance with their
specific religious beliefs? Surely some uniformity of religious belief
is a necessary pre-condition of effective religious education. No such
conformity seems to exist today which might be considered acceptable as a basis for religious education in state schools. Would it not
be wiser to omit religious education from the curriculum altogether?
Moral education seems a very attractive substitute. Is moral education enough?

John Wilson has made a courageous effort to apply rigorous logical analysis to the problems of moral education. The work of the
research unit is still at an early stage but the limitations of their
initial approach are already evident. A few quotations may illustrate
the difficulty. In his general introduction Wilson states:

Hence any 'basis for moral education' should consist of imparting those skills which are necessary to make good or reasonable moral decisions and to act on them. We are not out to impart any specific *content*, but to give other people facility in a *method*. This is what eventually happened with science, and this is why science and education in science eventually prospered: and this is what must happen to morality. Such an approach does not deny that we have moral knowledge now, any more that we would deny that the Middle Ages had scientific knowledge: but it does involve trying first to reach agreement about the second-order principles governing morality, rather than about what should be the (first-order) content of particular moral beliefs.[2]

This first quotation deserves analysis. It belongs to a context in which a parallel is being drawn between science and morality. The claim is being made that progress in moral education, like progress in scientific education, will depend primarily on 'facility in a method'. Agreement on 'second-order principles governing morality' must precede consideration of the appropriate content of moral beliefs. This is doubtless a sound order of procedure. It is certainly desirable, indeed essential, to expose the numerous fallacies in current talk about moral education. Wilson has used the techniques of logical analysis very helpfully. He has produced a set of 'second-order norms' which can be used to test the validity of moral argument. He has provided a set of rules for the 'language-game' of morality.

There is an important distinction, however, between morality and science. The logic of scientific method operates in a field where new insight can be tested objectively. Insights reached by using the 'second order norms' of morality cannot be tested in the same way. Ramsey's test of 'empirical fit' might seem appropriate here but it is, as we have seen, a subjective test. Ramsey's rules for the language-game of traditional Christian theology are only meaningful for those who have made a Christian commitment of the traditional type. What about Wilson's second-order norms for the language-game of morality? Would everyone be willing to play *that* game?

Wilson's answer to this question exposes the limitations of his linguistic approach. His book does not discuss the content of moral knowledge but there are one or two sentences which reveal the basic problem. Wilson writes:

There is no doubt a corpus of moral knowledge handed down by tradition, of whose validity we have every right to feel certain: and no doubt there are certain facts, contingent but not purely accidental, about the nature of human beings which can be used as a basis for the 'primary rules' in morality, or could be called 'natural law'. . . . Hence, while it is correct to say that one's rules and standards must be one's own, and not accepted uncritically from authority, it is not correct to say that one can do without standards altogether – unless one wishes to resign one's humanity and live at random. . . . As far as I can see at present, I would say that abandoning these norms means resigning from being a person.[3]

Wilson is claiming that the game of morality is a game which everyone must play. The rules of the game, when they have been clearly stated, belong to the very nature of human reason. Everyone who is truly a person must be expected to play the game of morality in accordance with the criteria which belong to rational discourse. Those who play the game according to these rules – the 'second-order norms' – would presumably reach ultimate agreement about the 'primary rules': thus a system of 'natural law' would be established securely. But what *is* a person? What are the 'facts about the nature of human beings' which can be used as a basis for the primary rules in morality?

Wilson's linguistic approach finds substantial support in R. S. Peters' *Ethics and Education*. In his introduction Peters draws attention to the possibilities and the limits of philosophical thinking on educational topics. He reminds us that 'during the twentieth century philosophy has been undergoing a revolution which has consisted largely in an increasing awareness of what philosophy is and is not'.[4] Philosophers have been compelled to abandon any claim to provide 'high-level directives for education or for life'. Their task is a humbler one. Their main function is 'the disciplined demarcation of concepts, the patient explication of the grounds of knowledge and of the presuppositions of different forms of discourse'.[5]

At a later point in his book Peters draws attention to the influence which man's understanding of his own nature exerts on human action. 'Men are unique amongst animals in many ways, but perhaps one of the most important features of their life is that its form is influenced enormously by the concept which they have of themselves. Their concept of man is one of the most important and far-reaching threads in the fabric of the public tradition into which they are initiated.'[6] He tells us that traditional concepts of man are 'culture-bound'. They 'enshrine the valuations of those who propound them'.[7] He argues that this need not be so. It may be possible to reach 'higher level generalizations about man which may be true universally'.[8] He then concludes:

The fundamental task, therefore, that remains to be tackled by those who wish to advance both educational and political theory is to get down to work in the philosophy of mind, in conjunction with psychologists, social scientists, historians, and men of wide practical experience and sound judgment. The time has passed when philosophers could, with a clear conscience, spin theories of human nature out of their own observations and introspection.[9]

Peters supports Wilson's view that the game of morality is a game which all human beings must play. He writes:

Many have, perhaps mistakenly, given up using religious language, for instance, because they have been brought to see what its use commits them to, e.g. saying things which purport to be true for which the truth conditions can never be produced. But it would be a very difficult position to adopt in relation to moral discourse, for it would entail a resolute refusal to talk or think about what ought to be done, which could constitute an abdication from a form of thought into which all in our society are initiated in varying degree.[10]

Peters does not venture to discuss the basic characteristics of human nature. He does not offer any answer to the question 'What is a person?', but there are one or two sentences in his book which suggest the lines along which his own thought is moving. Here are some which seem significant:

Any reflective person who asks the question 'Why do this rather than that?' cannot arbitrarily limit the context in which this question is asked. If he asks this question seriously he must answer it in the consciousness that there are regularities in nature, one of them being his own mortality as a man . . . In so far as he can stand back from his life and *ask* the question 'Why this rather than that?' he must already have a serious concern for truth built into his consciousness. . . . This attitude is not simply one of curiosity. It is rather the attitude of passionate concern for truth that informed Socrates' saying that the unexamined life is not worth living. . . . Such an attitude is surely in some way called forth by man's predicament as a thinking being in a universe whose local conditions have made thinking possible.[11]

Such sentences give fuller content to Wilson's comment that there are 'certain facts . . . about the nature of human beings which can be used as a basis for the primary rules of morality'. They point along the path which must be followed if we are to find 'higher generalizations about man which may be true universally'.[12] This path leads beyond the secure territory of linguistic analysis towards the frontiers of the unknown – the area once cultivated by metaphysicians. Those who venture out into that neglected area must certainly use the knowledge and insight of specialists in many fields – as the great philosophers have always done – but the pioneering must be done by individuals. 'Higher level generalizations' about human nature cannot be reached by majority vote in a committee of eminent specialists from a variety of related fields.

Martin Heidegger is a leading figure among those contemporary philosophers who have tried to follow this path. His analysis of the nature and conditions of human existence suggests that religion, as well as morality, belongs to the very structure of man's existence as a finite being. There is an inescapable dimension of mystery in human existence. Traditional religious language may not be meaningful for modern adolescents. We may need to learn a new language in order to discuss age-old themes, but the themes themselves may be valid and meaningful. Religion, like morality, may have its roots in the nature of man.

Before we examine Heidegger's analysis it would be fair to acknowledge the truth of Wilson's second contention. Uncertainty and confusion among religious believers was the second reason for the research unit's decision to undertake independent research on moral education. Uncertainty and confusion certainly exist. There are contemporary Christian writers who seem to ignore the dimension of mystery in human experience. They wish to 'secularize' the Christian faith. They remind us of Dietrich Bonhoeffer's plea for a *religionless* Christianity. The following passage from *Letters and Papers from Prison* has been quoted frequently:

Religious people speak of God when human perception is (often just from laziness) at an end, or human resources fail: it is in fact always the *Deus ex machina* they call to their aid, either for the solving of insoluble problems or as support in human failure – always, that is to say, helping out human weakness or on the borders of human existence. . . . I should like to speak of God not on the borders of life but at its centre, not in weakness but in strength, not, therefore, in man's suffering and death but in his life and prosperity. On the borders it seems to me better to hold our peace and leave the problem unsolved. Belief in the Resurrection is not the solution of the problem of death.[13]

The sentence, 'On the borders it seems to me better to hold our peace and leave the problem unsolved', sounds like an echo of

Wittgenstein's saying: 'Whereof one cannot speak, thereof one must be silent.'

The contemporary cult of 'religionless Christianity' has many vocal and persuasive adherents. All of them recognize that the traditional 'supernaturalism' of popular Christian belief is dead. Some of them have been seized by some new insight into an aspect of Christian truth. They have 'proved it upon their pulses', in John Keats' phrase, and they write of it with one-sided emphasis but with conviction and persuasive power. Some give the impression of seeking escape from the waters of unbelief on a shallow and leaky raft. It would be unfair to fix a common label on the numerous contemporary writers who have rejected traditional supernaturalism and are exploring new ways in Christian thinking. They vary greatly in depth and range of insight but many of them focus their thought on Jesus and neglect the dimension of human experience towards which the word *God* points. Such writers represent a significant Christian response to the secularizing tendency of modern culture and they have had their influence on religious education.

Does religionless Christianity offer a way towards the solution of our problems in religious education? Should we recognize frankly that the word *God* has ceased to be a meaningful word in contemporary life? *God*, in the traditional sense of the word, is dead. He belongs now to the borders of human existence. There we meet mystery and it is appropriate to be silent. The Church should stand, said Bonhoeffer, 'not where human powers give out, on the borders, but in the centre of the village'. Does that mean that religious education, in the traditional sense, should be abandoned? Should we cease talking about God and help our pupils to face the problems of everyday living? Are 'life themes' and 'real life situations' the key to religious education in the modern world? Should religious education be secularized? Is moral education enough? Such questions must be discussed more fully later.

Let us recognize, meantime, that Bonhoeffer's more radical disciples ignore the genuinely religious depths of Bonhoeffer's thought and life. An English officer who was a fellow-prisoner with Bonhoeffer in the closing weeks of his life wrote: 'Bonhoeffer was one of the few men I have ever known whose God was real and close to him.' He described the scene when Bonhoeffer was being taken to the scaffold. 'We bade him good-bye – he drew me aside. "This is the end," he said, "for me the beginning of life." '[14] It is against such a background that we must understand Bonhoeffer's words about religionless Christianity. Bonhoeffer knew that 'belief in the Resurrection is not the solution of the problem of death'. He believed that in the face of death it is 'better to hold our peace and leave the problem unsolved'. But he did not evade the thought of death and he was not haunted by the fear of death. When his last hours came he was sustained by the heritage of Christian belief and by his own deep and mature Christian faith.

Bonhoeffer did not quarrel with religion but with religiosity. Some of his words have the exaggeration characteristic of revolt. They are a clear call to mature Christian thinking and living but they do not offer a blueprint for a new secular Christianity. Religionless Christianity can be a way of escape from reality – a way of escape from the mystery at the heart of human existence. We do more honour to Bonhoeffer by responding to his call for maturity in Christian thought and life. Bonhoeffer knew that his faith offered no 'solution of the problem of death' but death had lost its power over him. He had already experienced 'eternal life' and he looked for the fulfilment of his Christian inheritance. He had learned to live trustfully and he was ready to die trustfully.

Brigid Brophy's polemical Fabian pamphlet *Religious Education in State Schools* (1966) raises the question 'How should we teach our children morality?' She answers: 'Exercise them in reason, and turn them loose on works of imaginative literature.' It is a good answer but it conceals two important questions. The first concerns the limitations of reason in assessing and guiding moral judgment and behaviour. The second concerns the deeper levels of human experience which find expression in the great imaginative literature of mankind. Both questions lead us in the same direction.

We have already found that consideration of the place of reason in moral judgment brings us to the threshold of profound questions about the nature of man and the conditions of human existence. Examination of the great imaginative literature of mankind brings us to the same threshold. Such a statement hardly needs to be illustrated. A great writer makes us deeply aware of the harsh discords and the rich harmonies in our human situation.

> The troubles of our proud and angry dust
> Are from eternity and shall not fail,

wrote Housman. Shakespeare expressed the same thought in the

familiar words of Macbeth: 'And all our yesterdays have lighted
fools the way to dusty death.' In another mood Shakespeare hinted
at a harmony in which discords might be resolved:

> . . . Men must endure
> Their going hence, even as their coming hither:
> Ripeness is all.

Such passages offer little consolation for troubled humanity but
they are nevertheless deeply religious in the true sense of that word.
They bring us face to face with the enduring realities of our human
situation as finite beings in a world we did not plan and cannot
control. Traditional religion has often served as a way of escape
from such realities, but it is by trustful response to them that
religious faith reaches maturity. In the words of Simone Weil:
'Everything that is threatened by time secretes falsehood in order
not to die . . . that is why there is not any love of truth without
an unconditional acceptance of death. The cross of Christ is the
only gateway to knowledge.'[15]

5 The Dimension of Mystery in Human Experience

John Dewey is said to have described agnosticism as 'the shadow cast by the eclipse of the supernatural'. It was a penetrating comment in its period but it is less apposite in a modern context. The agnostic of that definition was a man who professed ignorance on a question which has ceased to be meaningful today. The old question 'Does God exist?' is no longer valid in ordinary educated discussion. It raises too many prior philosophical questions. The 'supernatural' of traditional religion casts no shadow on the thoughts of modern man. It has ceased to exist.

Has the word 'mystery' become the last refuge of the wistful agnostic? Mystery casts a comfortable shadow within which former beliefs may lurk unnoticed. The shadow's outlines are vague and nebulous. Its source is quite undefined. Mystery is an emotive word which repels critical analysis yet such an analysis is needed before it can be used legitimately in discussing personal development.

Two quotations from Bernard Berenson's *Sunset and Twilight* may provide a starting point for such an analysis. The book consists mainly of selections from diaries written in the last ten years of the art critic's long life. Born a Jew, Berenson had been baptized into the Roman Catholic Church but he had rejected all religious belief in adult life. In his closing years he described his 'hostility to Christian theology in general and to Catholic in particular. It overshadows ritual, which in all churches has formed in the course of the ages the way for the poor human heart to cry its anguish, but also with the second Isaiah the comfort of aspiration . . . I feel the mystery of existence, and above all of awareness, every day of my life, and am too much in awe of it to talk glibly of a God, his intentions, purposes, and preferences.'[1] In an earlier passage he wrote: 'I no longer believe in a reality other than the one I am living. I no longer conceive of an explanation of the universe or our destiny or mission that would satisfy me, comfort me, bring "the troubled spirit" to rest.'[2]

Was Berenson an agnostic in Dewey's sense of the word? These extracts from his diary seem to support a negative answer to that question. The diary as a whole confirms that impression. His rejection of traditional Christian theology was too explicit and too persistent. The old 'supernatural' had lost all meaning for him. It had ceased to exist. Had 'mystery' taken the place of 'God'? Was it a comfortable refuge for emotions which could not find satisfaction in traditional religious beliefs? This question is much more difficult to answer. An affirmative answer would raise further questions. Are the conditions of human existence such that the human spirit *needs* channels of expression for 'anguish' and 'aspiration'? If this be so it must then be asked whether personal growth towards maturity is helped or hindered by the closing of such channels. Is the need for expressing such emotions a mark of immaturity? Is the appropriate expression of them an essential element in man's development towards maturity? Can we eliminate the dimension of mystery from human experience? If not, can we define it, and describe man's appropriate response to it in ways which leave no ground for critical comment?

Berenson's diaries show clearly that an awareness of mystery can persist as a central element in the experience of a man who has rejected all religious dogma. Ludwig Wittgenstein did not hesitate to acknowledge the 'mystical' although he left no rules for the language game of theology. Bertrand Russell, too, might be cited in support of the thesis that the dimension of mystery is a central and significant element in human experience. In *The Autobiography of Bertrand Russell: 1872-1914* he quotes extracts from correspondence with G. Lowes Dickinson in which he writes:

Seriously, the unmystical, rationalistic view of life seems to me to omit all that is most important and most beautiful. . . . But what we have to do, and what privately we do do, is to treat the religious instinct with profound respect, but to insist that there is no shred or particle of truth in any of the metaphysics it has suggested: to palliate this by trying to bring out the beauty of the world and of life, so far as it exists, and above all to insist upon preserving the seriousness of the religious attitude and its habit of asking ultimate questions.[3]

Human experience awakens depths of feeling which seek suitable channels of expression. The great religions of mankind have, in the past, provided such channels for the great majority of mankind. Art, music, literature and 'the consolations of philosophy' have provided them for others. The decay of traditional religious belief and practice have closed the religious channels for many thoughtful people today. But the need remains. The 'mystical' still 'shows itself' in moments of deeper experience. Human life grows shallow and trivial, personal development is starved and thwarted when such moments are ignored or evaded. Appropriate response to the dimension of mystery is a vital element in man's growth from birth to maturity.

The experimental scientist distrusts references to a dimension of mystery in human life. He regards it as an attempt to mark out an area of human experience from which scientific enquiry should be excluded. It seems to him like a rearguard engagement in the long struggle between reason and religious faith. His fears are justifiable. The phrase may sometimes be a mere cloak for ignorance and superstition. It may be cloudy rhetoric disguising emotional adherence to beliefs which reason can no longer accept. It may be a refuge from the chill winds of reason. But it need not be so. The scientist is right in refusing to acknowledge an iron curtain of religious prejudice beyond which he must not penetrate, but true mystery is deepened by advancing knowledge. It purges man's emotional nature from self-regarding motives. We may ignore it but we cannot ultimately escape from it. It belongs to the temporal structure of human existence.

Martin Heidegger's philosophical writings help to clarify and interpret the place of mystery in human experience. Heidegger was born in Germany in 1889. His major work was published in 1927 and passed through seven editions before it appeared in an English translation in 1962. The German editions had a wide and deep influence on European thought but Heidegger's influence in this country has been largely indirect until recent years. The title of the English translation, *Being and Time*, is a direct translation of the German *Sein und Zeit*. Reading the English translation is like reading Shakespeare. We frequently recognize quotations. It is not verbal expressions that we recognize, however, but the substance of his thought. His influence on the English speaking world may have been largely indirect but it has penetrated our contemporary idiom to a remarkable degree.

Heidegger's main interest lies in the problem of Being. 'Why is there anything at all? Why is there not just nothing?' This question, posed by Leibniz, leads us directly to his central problem. The mystery of Being lies at the heart of his philosophical enquiries. The title, *Being and Time*, shows the direction in which these enquiries moved. Heidegger recognized that the temporal nature of human experience imposed a limit on man's understanding of Being. The human intellect cannot pass beyond the frontiers of temporal experience. On the other hand, man *knows* that his experience has temporal limits. He knows that he must die. That very fact enables man to reflect on the nature of temporal existence and, perhaps, to recognize more clearly the impossibility of finding an answer to Leibniz's question. Being may remain mysterious but the nature of the mystery may be clarified.

Heidegger approaches his problem through an analysis of human existence. He believes that man's self-awareness opens a window through which the nature of being begins to be disclosed. Human existence differs from all other modes of being in this fact of self-awareness. Man lives, decides and acts in the present but he is aware of the past and he is mindful of the future. Past, present and future belong together in human experience. Human existence derives its unique character from this fact. 'Man only casts the image of his joys beyond his sense's reach,' wrote Cecil Day Lewis. When man is true to his own nature he cannot be content to live at the instinctive level like the animals. 'I wish I could turn and live with the animals, they're placid and self-contained,' wrote Walt Whitman. But we cannot do so. Responsibility towards the future – what Heidegger calls care – with its prevailing mood of anxiety is of the very essence of human existence.

Heidegger finds three aspects in man's awareness of time. The first relates to the future. Man is never a complete being. His nature is not determined at any point in his existence. The future is always open and human decisions help to shape it. 'The thoughts of youth are long, long thoughts,' wrote Longfellow. In youth the world is at our feet and, in our dreams at least, the possibilities before us seem limitless. But that is only one aspect of man's temporal experience. Even youth, in more sober moments, knows that such dreams of the future have little substance. Shades of the prison house begin to close around us. We must face the second aspect in our awareness of time. That aspect relates to the past. We are limited by our past – by genetic endowment, by social inheritance, by early experiences – by the 'thrownness' of human existence, as Heidegger calls it. We find ourselves thrown into the midst of existence and we have to sink or swim. Some of us are male, some are female. Some are tall and some are short. Some are clever and some are not so clever. Some grow up in a comfortable, cultured home. Some know poverty and hardship from their earliest years. Some are reared in love and security. Others are exposed to tensions and fears from birth. All this, and much else, belongs to the 'thrownness' of human existence.

The third aspect in our awareness of time concerns the present. We seek to disown the limitations imposed by our past. We are unwilling to face the responsibilities of the future. We continually seek escape from past and future into the fleeting interests of the passing moment. This, too, is characteristic of human existence. Heidegger calls this aspect in our awareness of time 'fallenness'. *Possibility, thrownness, fallenness*: these three characteristics of human existence affect man's responsibility for the future. They have their roots in man's awareness of time.

Death has a special place in Heidegger's analysis of human existence. It is an essential element in man's awareness of time and it is related to each aspect of temporal awareness. It belongs to the future as a limiting possibility. It is a possibility, in Heidegger's sense, because we must relate ourselves to it in one way or another. Death itself is a certainty but men relate themselves to that certainty in many ways. At any moment of time man's existence is incomplete and he must relate himself to all the possibilities which life may still hold for him. The manner in which he does so affects his growth towards personal maturity, towards completeness as a human being, towards 'Being a whole', in Heidegger's phrase. Death is, in this sense, the ultimate and inescapable possibility.

Death belongs also to the past. It is part of our human inheritance. It belongs to the 'thrownness' of human existence. Death is not an accidental possibility which may happen to some but not to others. It belongs to man's experience of living. To live, as a human being, is to live with death as a constant, and ultimately inescapable, possibility.

Death belongs to the present also. Man decides and acts in the present and death is a future possibility which must affect his present living. 'Fallenness' is the characteristic which Heidegger finds in man's relationship to the present. It shows itself, in face of death, by absorption in the present. This enables man to escape from the thought of death. Heidegger's discussion of the significance of death for human existence provides a focal point for his important distinction between *authentic* and *inauthentic* living.

Authentic existence in face of death is *responsible* existence. It is characterized by care with its prevailing mood of anxiety. The familiarity of these words in common speech is apt to obscure their special significance in Heidegger's terminology. An old Quaker saying may help to make Heidegger's meaning clearer. 'There is a carelessness which is blameworthy. There is a higher carelessness which is a gift of God.' There is also a kind of care and a kind of anxiety which are blameworthy. They spring from ego-centric motives. But there is a higher kind of care and anxiety which are the mark of responsible human living. Ego-centric motives have been subdued and even death can be accepted without neurotic evasion or neurotic brooding.

Authentic existence in face of death is marked by *freedom*. This word can also be misleading. There is a false freedom which can be found through absorption in passing interests. This is the freedom of 'flight from reality' in Freud's phrase. It is the freedom offered by drug-taking in all its forms – material and non-material – by any type of human experience which offers forgetfulness. A. E. Housman's lines are relevant here:

> Could man be drunk for ever,
> With liquor, love or fights,
> Lief should I rouse at morning
> And lief lie down of nights.
>
> But men at whiles are sober
> And think by fits and starts,
> And if they think, they fasten
> Their hands upon their hearts.[4]

This is inauthentic freedom – and it does not last. Authentic freedom in face of death is only possible when ego-centric concern has been overcome.

Authentic existence in face of death is characterized also by serenity. Heidegger uses the words *joy*, *elation* and *equanimity* in his attempts to express this mood. This mood 'springs from resoluteness which, in a moment of vision, looks at those situations which are possible in one's potentiality-for-Being-a-whole as disclosed in one's anticipation of death'.[5] The key phrase, 'One's potentiality-for-Being-a-whole', deserves closer examination. It may be linked with the important human question: 'Who am I?' We are all so many different people. We are subject to conflicting moods. We would fain repudiate actions which we ourselves have done. How can we interpret selfhood? Heidegger interprets it in temporal terms.

True selfhood is always a future possibility. Past, present and future enter into every moment of experience and have a bearing on our attitudes, decisions and actions. Inauthentic existence means losing one's potential unity through immersion in each fleeting moment. The individual is at the mercy of changing circumstances and mass opinions. Paul had a helpful way of describing this. He called it being like 'children, tossed to and fro, and carried about with every wind of doctrine' (Eph. 4.14). He called it also being 'conformed to this world' (Rom. 12.2). The individual lives in a world of false security and wishful thinking. Past, present and future are not related realistically to one another.

Authentic existence involves holding past, present and future together in a unity of experience. In this experience man's 'potentiality-for-Being-a-whole' – for achieving the unity of true selfhood – begins to emerge. Authentic existence is marked by resoluteness of will. The individual maintains awareness of all the possibilities which belong to the totality of human existence, including the ultimate, inescapable possibility of death. The moment of vision in which past and future are held together in the authentic present is a moment of joy, elation, equanimity – or serenity. In such moments man glimpses the unity of true selfhood. In such unity the whole self decides and acts responsibly, freely and serenely. This unity is an ideal possibility towards which human living may gradually approximate. At the same time it is the true norm of human existence.

There is an obvious parallel between Heidegger's analysis of authentic living and Paul's account of Christian living. When Rudolf Bultmann tried to demythologize the New Testament and express the gospel in contemporary language he used Heidegger's distinction between authentic and inauthentic living. Heidegger is often driven to use paradox in discussing the distinction between authentic and inauthentic living. Man must live in the present but he must not be absorbed by the present. Paul also writes paradoxically. We find him using the indicative and the imperative mood side by side in his letters. 'You have been raised with Christ,' he wrote to the Christians at Colossae. This is a confident affirmation. Paul is using the indicative mood. He is reminding the Colossian Christians that they share the perfect resurrection life of Christ. Later in the passage the mood changes: 'set your mind on things that are above.' This is moral exhortation and the passage continues in the imperative mood. Perfection is the norm of Christian living, for Paul, but it is an ideal possibility towards which Christian living can only approximate by successive acts of response to divine grace. Authentic living is also, for Heidegger, a norm and an ideal possibility.

How is authentic living possible? How can the potential unity of the whole self be progressively attained? In *Being and Time* Heidegger leaves the impression that authentic existence can be realized by consistent and resolute direction of the human will. In later writing he reveals, more openly, a mystical element in his thought. He claims that traditional western thought has been too rationalistic. He wants to return to the pre-Socratic roots of western philosophy where he finds a type of thinking in which truth is disclosed to the submissive and responsive mind. Heidegger finds a significant link between three similar German words: *denken*, to think; *danken*, to thank; and *dichten*, to compose poetry. He claims that philosophical thinking (*denken*) should share the qualities of religious devotion (*danken*) and poetic expression (*dichten*). Truth is not mastered by human reason. It is disclosed to the whole man in moments of submissive response.[6]

The question of Leibniz, 'Why is there anything at all? Why is there not just nothing?', is not one which can be answered by traditional metaphysical thinking. It is a question which awakens wonder and a sense of mystery. In doing so it may prepare us to respond to the gracious self-disclosure of Being. Heidegger would not equate Being with God in the traditional sense of that word but his thought is clearly moving in a religious dimension. His analysis of human existence discloses the centrality and significance of death in human experience but it does not end negatively in fatalistic despair and the levelling out of all human values. It ends positively. Acceptance of the conditions of human existence – including death – contains the possibility of self-fulfilment through submissive response to the mystery of Being.

Here we reach a frontier beyond which human thought cannot

take us. Man must respond submissively to ultimate mystery. Being gives itself to man, says Heidegger. Wittgenstein, the father of linguistic analysis, committed himself to a similar statement: 'There is indeed the inexpressible. This *shows* itself; it is the mystical.'[7] He also said: 'Not *how* the world is, is the mystical but *that* it is.'[8] Wittgenstein, too, reminds us of the mystery of Being.

Heidegger's most important contribution to the contemporary problems of religious education lies in his recognition of the significance of death for our understanding of human existence. Awareness of death gives depth to human experience. It awakens man to the dimension of mystery. This is the religious dimension of human life. Man may respond to this experience of mystery in two ways. He may accept it and live with it trustfully. He may reject it and flee from it in anxious fear. The manner in which he responds colours the whole pattern of his living. Existentialist writers have been criticized sometimes, by Bonhoeffer among others, for morbid preoccupation with death. But refusal to acknowledge the reality of death may be just as morbid. More than one contemporary writer has drawn attention to the conspiracy of silence about death which has replaced the conspiracy of silence about sex. Silence and incessant talk are equally symptomatic of morbid immaturity in these two emotionally sensitive areas of human experience. The breakdown of Victorian reticence about sex at least opened the door to a more mature attitude to human relationships. Frank recognition of death might open the door to greater maturity in the religious dimension of life.

How can we promote personal development from infancy through childhood and adolescence to the maturity of true selfhood? *The Problem Child at Home* by Mary Buell Sayles (Commonwealth Fund Publications, 1928) was published more than forty years ago and was widely read at that time. It was an early contribution to the practical problems of personal development in children. It named three basic emotional needs of the growing child: security, freedom for personal growth and a concrete pattern of human living. Security was presented as the most fundamental need and love was stressed as the essential condition of security. Many volumes have been written since then, practical and theoretical, popular and profound, on the theme of personal development. The need for security and the importance of love have been stressed again and again. The meaning of these two words has been clarified and deepened. Love has been described in ways that come very close to the New Testament meaning of that word. One contemporary psychiatrist acknowledges that the kind of love which children need from their parents and patients need from psychiatrists can only be described appropriately by the New Testament word *agape*. Another acknowledges that this completely satisfying love relationship is only an ideal possibility. It is never realized in actual fact.

Why is this so? Why cannot parents, teachers, even psychiatrists, provide the security of love in full perfection? We might follow Heidegger's analysis of human existence and recognize that 'fallenness' is part of the structure of man's temporal existence. Man shrinks from responsible living. He is unwilling to accept the limitations of his human heritage and to face responsibly the possibilities of his future. 'Fallenness' is a characteristic of human existence and it is transmitted, perhaps, from generation to generation by social inheritance.

We might turn from Heidegger to the Bible and reflect on the old Hebrew myth of the Fall. What does that story mean? More than one interpretation is possible, but it is surely significant that the serpent encourages the woman to distrust her Maker. The serpent 'said to the woman, "Did God say, 'You shall not eat of any tree of the garden?'" And the woman said to the serpent, "We may eat of the fruit of the trees of the garden; but God said, 'You shall not eat of the tree which is in the midst of the garden, neither shall you touch it, lest you die.'" But the serpent said to the woman, "You will not die. For God knows that when you eat of it your eyes will be opened, and you will be like God, knowing good and evil"' (Gen. 3.1-4). God was hiding his real motive, suggested the serpent. He could not be trusted. He was not trying to save man from death. He was trying to prevent man winning the knowledge and power which belong properly to God alone. Disobedience had its roots in distrust. So the old myth declares. The myth of Genesis, and the existential analysis of Heidegger, see 'fallenness', in two distinct but not unrelated senses, as part of the structure of man's temporal existence. Man is just like that. The Christian doctrine of salvation sees divine love, the perfect *agape*, as the source of healing and renewal. Heidegger seems to point tentatively in the same direction when he speaks of submissive response to the mystery of Being.

Man's 'fallenness' is the source of adult failure in all human relationships. There are no perfect parents, perfect teachers or perfect psychiatrists because there are no perfect human beings. What can we do, then, to help boys and girls in their development towards personal maturity? Here we come to the crux of our problem. This is the point at which Christians and humanists part company. Christians would emphasize the supernatural power of divine grace and would urge the importance of full Christian education. Humanists would press for moral education without indoctrination into any particular religious belief or even into a religious interpretation of life. Can we build a bridge between the two positions?

'Is Being gracious?' is the question which John Macquarrie would wish us to substitute for the misleading question 'Does God exist?'[9] God certainly does not exist as sticks and stones, the count less stellar systems of outer space, or the human beings on this tiny satellite of an insignificant solar system exist. He is not a bit of the universe. Can we live trustfully in awareness of the mystery of the universe? Is Being trustworthy? Is Being gracious? Heidegger would seem to give a positive answer. Other existentialists, like Sartre, would disagree. Christians would answer positively and would rest their confidence on certain happenings in history – on their interpretation of a life lived and a death died. This is the Christian 'leap of faith'. It provides adequate ground for full Christian education within the community of Christian believers. Does it justify a Christian minority in imposing a full Christian education on the children of non-Christian parents? Is a full Christian education possible without the support of a believing community? Is there a legitimate place for religious education in the state school?

Heidegger's analysis of human existence suggests a first step towards an answer to such questions. There is a religious dimension – a dimension of mystery – in human experience which we cannot ignore when we think seriously about personal development. True selfhood can only be attained when man learns to live trustfully in awareness of the mystery. It would seem to follow that this dimension of mystery cannot be ignored when we plan an educational curriculum. In the opening paragraphs of his *Introduction to Metaphysics* (Oxford: O.U.P., 1959) Heidegger quotes Leibniz's question: 'Why is there anything at all? Why is there not just nothing?' He suggests that everyone may be 'grazed at least once by the hidden power of this question' even if it does not become fully conscious and articulate. Leibniz put the question in a sophisticated philosophical form. A group of boys and girls in their adolescence prepared some questions to which they wanted answers. The first was: 'How should we view our lives here on earth? What is the purpose of a human life?' The second was: 'What is the meaning of human death?' They would not have understood Leibniz's question but they had been 'grazed' by its power. Awareness of such questions gives depth and poignancy to human living. They have their source in the very nature of human existence. Christians and non-Christians could surely agree on a common intention to recognize this dimension of mystery in educational planning.

Can a further step be taken towards a common policy? All educators would agree that an environment of love is essential for healthy human development. Many of all shades of opinion would agree that the life and death of Jesus have been the supreme example and inspiration of self-forgetful love in our western tradition. Donald Mackinnon, the Christian theologian, and Antony Flew, who would probably describe himself as an agnostic or atheist, once engaged in a debate on religious questions. A few sentences from their discussion seem relevant:

D.M. . . . in this riddle of Christ's life lived and Christ's death died we see through a glass darkly the infinite boundless love, love without condition, translated into terms of the finite and the bounded.
A.F. I agree entirely that this is the heart of the matter and I will try to return here . . . The heart of the matter is that the only satisfactory and the perhaps sufficient justification for the whole enterprise of trying to say things which it seems necessarily cannot be said lies just there; in Christ: 'In the riddle of a life lived and a death died.'[10]

Would a non-partisan study of Christian origins be acceptable as one element in a common policy for religious education in state schools?

6 Religion and Personal Development

Over forty years ago Ernest Jones expressed the psycho-analytical view of religion in a vivid sentence. He was discussing the fruits of psycho-analytic study of religious belief and life over a period of twenty-five years. He wrote: 'The outstanding conclusion that emerges from all this investigation is that *the religious life represents a dramatization on a cosmic plane of the emotions, fears and longings which arose in the child's relation to his parents.*'[1] Freud's own book *The Future of an Illusion* expounded this same theme. Religious beliefs are 'illusions, fulfilments of the oldest, strongest and most insistent wishes of mankind.'[2] Religious belief and practice is 'wish-fulfilment'.

Christian apologists have recovered from the shock of such statements but Christian thinkers have not always admitted their positive significance. It has been recognized and emphasized that psychologists, of whatever school, cease to write as psychologists when they pass judgment on the validity of beliefs whose psychological origins they have been discussing. Even Freud himself is careful to define his use of the word illusion. 'We call a belief an illusion when wish-fulfilment is a prominent factor in its motivation, while disregarding its relations to reality.'[3] Nevertheless the Freudian attack on religion has important implications which merit careful consideration. It is as unwise to dismiss Freud's critique of religion as it is to quote Jung in support of religious belief. Both were careful to define the limits of their psychological investigations although each, at times, strayed beyond these limits.

Psychological investigation has certainly shown very clearly that personal development and religious development are intimately related. The conclusion to which Ernest Jones found himself led is valid within its own limits. Religious belief and practice reflect many levels of psychological maturity. The persistence of infantile

traits in personal development affects the substance of religious life.
The Swiss psycho-analyst and pastor Oskar Pfister's notable book,
Christianity and Fear (1949), supplied ample evidence of this claim.
Maturity in personal development is intimately associated with
maturity in religious development. Is the latter just one aspect of
the former? What is our criterion of personal maturity? Is a
'neurotic' St Teresa less mature than a serene untroubled Christian,
or humanist, who lives on the surface of life and has fewer glimpses
into its heights and depths? Is religion a helpful or harmful element
in personal development? Is personal maturity the true goal of
religious education? These are important and difficult questions
but they must not be ignored.

Erik Erikson's valuable study, *Childhood and Society*, provides
a most helpful introduction to the discussion of such topics. Erikson
has been Professor of Human Development and Lecturer on Psy-
chiatry at Harvard University since 1960. *Childhood and Society*
was his first book and it gained rapid recognition as an important
contribution to the problems of personal development in the setting
of social change. He exposes very clearly the interrelationship of
physical, mental and social factors in human life.

Erikson speaks of 'the basic sense of trust and the basic sense
of mistrust which remain the autogenic source of both primal hope
and doom throughout life'.[4] This is familiar ground. Trust and
distrust have figured in psychological discussion of personal development over many years. They entered into our discussion of authentic
and inauthentic living. Authentic living is trustful living. Inauthentic
living is rooted in distrust. Using Paul's language we might say that
the natural man is moved by ego-centric motives springing from
distrust while the Christian who responds to divine grace is being
delivered from ego-centric fears.

What has Erikson to say about the origins of trust and mistrust
in personal development? He traces the source of these two attitudes
back to the very beginning of the infant's independent physical
existence. The life of the newly born infant depends on its ability
to suck and on the availability of suitable food which can be secured
by sucking. In this initial situation the infant begins, normally, to
experience a trustworthy world and to respond trustfully, hopefully
and actively to it. Yet the satisfactions of infant experience are not
unbroken. There are always times of frustration, discomfort and
delayed satisfaction. Trust and mistrust, acceptance and rejection,

co-operation and rebellion, love and hate intermingle in the infant's responses to changing experiences from the earliest hours of life. Teething, weaning and toilet training raise new problems. Nature and society compel the infant to accept readjustments which involve effort and initiative. The infant's experience is no longer mainly pleasurable. Life ceases to seem wholly trustworthy. It includes bad experiences as well as good ones. The expulsion from paradise, from the 'dreaming innocence of undecided potentialities'[5] is inevitable. Personal decision is the birthright and the burden of human existence. The long slow journey towards personal maturity begins in the cradle.

Three factors affect the character of that journey. The first is a constitutional one.[6] There are individual differences due to biological inheritance, pre-natal influences and possible birth injuries. This first factor defines the possibilities of the newly born infant. The second is the social factor. The social pattern to which the infant is exposed exercises pressure on infant behaviour. This pressure operates first through nursery routine and, later, through the type of discipline and the consistency of adult standards which the child meets in the home and in his early school contacts. The third factor is individual response. The infant begins very early to develop his own characteristic way of responding to the experiences which life brings. The possibility of full personal decision is latent in these early responses.

We can relate these factors to Heidegger's analysis of human existence. There is first the 'throwness' of man's temporal existence. The newly-born infant starts off with certain possibilities and certain limitations which constitute his initial equipment for the journey of life. Later adverse or favourable individual circumstances must be included in these possibilities and limitations. Illness, accident, the loss of a parent, a broken home are typical of the adverse, external and fortuitous circumstances which can affect personal development. These, too, are part of the 'throwness' of human existence. It is true at every stage of life that the past cannot be altered.

There is, secondly, the openness characteristic of man's future. At every stage man is still an incomplete being. The past may be unalterable but the future is still uncharted. The factor of individual response begins at the organic level but it contains the possibility of full personal decision. Man is an incomplete being whose true norm lies in completeness, in wholeness, in the unity and integrity of personal maturity.

The third factor exposes the heart of the human problem. It is the 'fallenness' of human existence – as Heidegger calls it. The pattern of social belief and behaviour exercises pressure on the individual's responses and decisions from the very beginning. Progress towards maturity needs personal moral discipline. A stable social tradition fosters and sustains moral control by providing an acceptable pattern of human living. Such a pattern restrains egocentric demands and provides channels for the satisfaction of basic needs. A stable social tradition also fosters traditional attitudes towards the final mysteries of human existence.

Every pattern of social behaviour is, however, a complex web of human hopes and fears, trust and mistrust, hate and love. Social pressures and sanctions in the home, in the school and in adult life may restrain and control anti-social behaviour. They cannot cure the deep inner tensions and fears from which such behaviour springs. The pattern of social belief and behaviour helps to guide and to control individual response but it also transmits the 'fallenness' of human existence.

Erikson makes a significant comment on the function of institutional religion in social life. He writes: 'The parental faith which supports the trust emerging in the newborn has throughout history sought its institutional safeguard, and, on occasion, found its greatest enemy in organized religion.'[7] Erikson's cryptic and dogmatic statement can be supplemented and clarified by reference to Jung's well-known views on religion. Jung believed that institutional religion had a therapeutic function in human society. Religious belief and practice could provide relief from emotional tension which the individual was unable to face. It could provide a spiritual substitute for physical drugs. But Jung recognized clearly that this was a palliative and not a real cure. It might be a valuable palliative. It might prevent complete breakdown but it might leave the real problem unresolved. It might relieve the burden of neurotic fears and satisfy regressive longing for the security of childhood without really helping the individual towards fuller and richer personal life. It might remove the symptoms but leave the fundamental spiritual condition unchanged.

Jung was equally clear, however, that the journey to personal maturity had a religious dimension. He believed that it involved the reconciliation of conflicting elements within the personality. These views are illustrated very clearly in his account of a patient's dreams (*Psychology and Religion* and *The Integration of the Personality*). This man had been brought up in the Roman Catholic Church. He had reacted in adolescence against his early religious training and had adopted a sceptical rationalistic view of life. This solution had involved a sharp division in his personality. His conscious attitudes were rigid and limited in range. They were sharply separated from his emotional life, which remained immature and repressed.

When Jung met his patient this compromise solution of his adolescent problems had broken down in neurosis. The patient was in danger of seeking escape from his neurosis by swinging back to earlier attitudes. This would have left his real problem unresolved. Religion would have been a safety-valve for unsatisfied emotion. His condition would have remained neurotic and unstable. His dreams pointed to a richer solution. They dramatized his problem in vivid, and sometimes grotesque, symbols and they warned him against the danger of seeking to escape from conflict. The way of growth, towards which Jung was seeking to guide his patient, was indicated clearly by words which the patient heard at a particularly solemn moment in one of his dreams : 'A voice says "What thou art doing is dangerous . . . Woe to those who use religion as a substitute for the other side of the soul's life. They are in error and shall be cursed. Religion is no substitute, but it is the ultimate accomplishment added to every other activity of the soul. Out of the fulness of life thou shalt give birth to thy religion, only then shalt thou be blessed." '[8] The path to healing and wholeness led through conflict and reconciliation.

Jung dwelt frequently on the parallels between the healing process, as he met it in the experience of his patients, and the concepts of mystical religion. He found these parallels in esoteric Eastern sects but he also turned, at times, to the New Testament. He described the healing change which he had seen in the experience of his patients in the following sentences : 'the centre of gravity of the total personality shifts its position. It ceases to be in the ego . . . a change known to us through the confession of the Apostle Paul : "no longer do I live, but Christ liveth in me" . . . It is as if the leadership of the affairs of life had gone over to an invisible centre.'[9] Jung claimed that this change involved the most complete development of personality of which the individual was capable. It implied 'fidelity to the law of one's own being'.[10]

Traditional religious beliefs and practices offer guidance and direction for human living. They tell men what to believe and how to act. They provide a sheltering framework within which individuals may grow towards freedom in belief and action. But they also offer a way of escape from the loneliness of personal decision. They may help but they may also hinder man's growth towards personal maturity. When are they helpful and when do they hinder personal development?

Jung's views provide support for the argument that personal development has a religious dimension. They compel us, however, to face a question which has been raised already but not discussed. Jung recognized parallels between certain experiences of his patients and certain concepts of mystical religion. He found religious symbols figuring in the dreams of his patients. He was prepared to assert that these symbols were psychologically true but he was unwilling to comment on their 'metaphysical' status. He traced the origin of the symbols to the deeper levels of the unconscious mind but he was equally unwilling to comment on the metaphysical status of the unconscious and its contents. He admitted that 'the concept of the unconscious mind is a mere assumption for the sake of convenience'.[11]

Many of Jung's patients were less cautious. They denied the religious significance of symbols appearing in their dreams. They claimed that such symbols referred to changes and experiences within their own personality. Jung asserted, therefore, that for many modern minds 'the place of the deity seems to be taken by the wholeness of man'.[12] The attitude of such patients may be discounted. No doubt they were rejecting a religious interpretation of their experiences because traditional religious language had lost all meaning for them. Jung's own views touched a deeper level and they raise a sharper problem. Do theology and psychology just describe the same facts in two different languages? Does religious insight penetrate more deeply into reality than the insight of psychology? Is there any essential difference between psychological maturity and religious maturity?

There can be no neat and tidy answer to these questions. The exponents of 'religionless Christianity' are doubtless right in their claim that the coming of Christ abolished the distinction between sacred and secular in principle but they are surely wrong if they imply that it can be ignored in ordinary Christian practice. The complete abolition of that distinction is still only an ideal possibility and not a blueprint for everyday living. It belongs to the perfection of Christ's kingdom and that perfection is still an unrealized hope. It is not a present possession.

Heidegger's analysis of human existence provides a basis for acknowledging the dimension of mystery in human experience. Authentic existence is a convenient neutral term for defining the true norm and the ideal goal of human development but Christians and non-Christians will still differ regarding the appropriate path to the attainment of that goal. Most non-Christians would probably agree with the prevailing note in *Being and Time*. They would hold that authentic existence can only be attained – in so far as it is attainable – by resolute and persistent efforts of the human will. Christians would find themselves more in sympathy with the mystical element in Heidegger's later thought. They would emphasize the possibilities of growth towards the ideal by trustful response to divine grace. They would regard the teaching and the sacraments of the church as vital elements in the communication of healing and renewing grace.

Such differences explain, and justify, a difference of emphasis between religious education within the life of the church and religious education in a state school. Does this mean that the goal of religious education in a state school must be limited to a humanistic ideal of personal maturity? Such a claim would seem doctrinaire and impracticable. In the life of the spirit a neurotic tendency may be like the grain of sand in an oyster's shell. St Teresa's autobiography (*The Life of St Teresa*, London: Penguin Books, 1957) contains a great deal which psychologists might regard as evidence of neurotic tendencies, but it also reveals remarkable insight into the heights and depths of human experience. William Blake might also be called 'neurotic' but we do not dismiss his penetrating insights into the human situation. The criteria of psychological maturity have obvious limitations. Religious education would be impoverished if it were reduced to 'religionless' teaching.

Such teaching would also be impracticable. Most boys and girls are exposed to traditional religious beliefs and practices in some degree before they come to school. Some may continue to find help from traditional religion in their personal development. Some may gain depths of insight, within traditional religious belief and practice, which remain unknown to those outside. The final test, in psychological or in religious maturity, lies in freedom from the claims and burdens of ego-centricity. At the ideal level psychological and religious maturity may be indistinguishable. At the level of ordinary living it would be misleading to measure religious maturity by the standards of psychological maturity.

Erik Erikson's book (*Childhood and Society*) contains a thought-provoking chapter entitled 'Eight Ages of Man'. In it he attempts to define the characteristic tasks and achievements at eight stages in human development from birth to maturity. His account of the last stage contains some helpful comments. He reminds us that 'a favourable ratio of basic trust over basic mistrust is the first step in psychosocial adaptation',[13] but he makes it clear that this 'basic ratio' enters into, and is influenced by, each successive stage and crisis in the cycle of human development. Erikson uses the term 'ego integrity' to describe the final fruit of primal trust. 'In such final consolidation,' he writes, 'death loses its sting.'[14] 'Renunciation and wisdom' define the qualities associated with this final stage. Erikson suggests that the basic features of this stage are independent of cultural differences. 'Each individual, to become a mature adult, must to a sufficient degree develop all the ego qualities mentioned, so that a wise Indian, a true gentleman, and a mature peasant share and recognize in one another the final stage of integrity.'[15]

Primitive societies used initiation rites to control personal development through adolescence to full manhood and womanhood. In doing so they imposed a rigid pattern of belief and conduct on each successive generation but they also provided channels through which basic human needs and desires, hopes and fears might find expression. They provided guidance for belief and action in the three basic areas of human development: sex, society and 'the gods'. During the course of Christian history there have been periods of relative stability when social pressures served a similar function. Erikson seems to suggest that personal development towards maturity is not necessarily hindered by the severe pressures of initiation rites nor by the gentler pressures of social tradition. Personal freedom is still possible within the social pattern, freedom is only hampered when individuals grow beyond the traditional pattern. 'The final stage of integrity' can be attained within different types of social culture. The circumstances of man's temporal existence are the ultimate determining circumstances in his growth towards maturity. The decisive factor is the individual's response to these circumstances. Is it an attitude of open trustful acceptance or is it marked by distrust and withdrawal?

Erikson recognizes that contemporary culture poses special problems for personal development. He tells us that the psychiatrist of today is confronting a new type of human need which arises from the breakdown of stable moral and social traditions. 'The patient of today suffers most under the problem of what he should believe in and who he should – or, indeed, might – be or become; while the patient of early psychoanalysis suffered most under inhibitions which prevented him from being what and who he thought he knew he was.'[16] In an earlier generation patients were in revolt against the inhibiting chains of a decaying tradition. Now the tradition *has* decayed. A new type of patient is appearing who is perplexed and troubled by the demands of human freedom and personal choice. Who am I? What is the meaning of human existence? These questions disturb modern man because social tradition has broken down and traditional answers have ceased to be relevant.

The state schools of western society include pupils with very varied needs. Some need help in growing beyond inherited beliefs. Others need support in resolving the moral and intellectual dilemmas of an age which has lost moral clarity and religious conviction. Moral and religious education must satisfy both needs. Atheists and agnostics, Christians and humanists, Jews and Muslims share a common humanity. The problems of moral choice remain although religious sanctions have decayed. The dimension of mystery remains although traditional religious interpretations of the mystery have been outgrown and discarded. Pupils in our schools are conscious of the pressures of moral choice and ultimate belief. Traditional adult interpretations may often seem irrelevant but the pressures remain and the need for guidance remains.

State schools must face this responsibility seriously and realistically. Moral and religious education is a peculiarly difficult and delicate task in modern society, but moral and religious needs are still closely intertwined. Man's relationship to 'the gods' is still bound up with his relationship to his fellowmen. A 'favourable ratio of basic trust over basic mistrust' is the passport to healthy living at both levels. By encouraging the growth of trust and interpreting the meaning of love religious education can play a vital part in fostering growth towards the fullest maturity of which individual boys and girls may be capable.

7   The Crux of the Problem

Modern use of the term *religious education* reveals the crux of our educational problem. It suggests a false dichotomy. Religion and education both involve the whole man. They are not separable parts of some larger whole. In primitive society religion and education were each concerned with the whole of life. There were indeed certain beliefs and practices relating to the gods which had to be learned at adolescence. They required separate treatment, as social and sexual customs did, but they were not ultimately separable. They were woven into the intricate web of social and personal life.

When John Milton wrote his *Tractate on Education* in the seventeenth century he defined the aim of education in religious terms. 'The end then of education,' he wrote, 'is to repair the ruins of our first parents by regaining to know God aright.' These words have been quoted frequently but the words which follow are equally illuminating: 'But because our understanding cannot in this body found itself on sensible things, nor arrive so clearly to the knowledge of God and things invisible, as by orderly conning over the visible and inferior creature, the same method is necessarily to be followed in all discreet teaching.' Knowledge of the scriptures was a vital part of the educational curriculum but it was part of a larger whole. All knowledge had a religious dimension. All education was governed by a religious aim.

This view of education finds twentieth-century expression in the papal encyclical *Divini Illius Magistri* (1929).

It is therefore an extremely important matter to make no mistake in this question of education; as important, in fact, as it is to make no mistake in regard to man's final destiny, for it is to this that the entire work of education is necessarily directed. For if the whole purpose of education is so to shape man in this mortal life that he will be able to reach the last end for which his Creator has destined him, it is plain that there can be no true education which is not totally directed to that last end.[1]

The same document states the case for the church school.

For the mere fact that religious teaching (often very meagre) is imparted in a school does not make it satisfy the rights of the Church and the family nor render it fit to be attended by Catholic pupils. For this, the whole of the training and teaching, the whole organization of the school – teachers, curriculum, school-books on all subjects – must be so impregnated with the Christian spirit under the guidance and motherly vigilance of the Church, that religion comes to provide the foundation and the culminating perfection of the whole training.[2]

Traditional religious teaching within a school which is permeated by secular assumptions is a barren compromise. Education, like religion, is concerned with the whole of life. The term religious education suggests a false dichotomy.

In January 1934 the Student Christian Movement Press published the first number of a new quarterly review with the title *Religion in Education*. The opening editorial made a brief but significant comment on the title: 'No more need be said in explanation of our title "Religion in Education" save that it implies education in religion, and this on the highest level of technical excellence, as the greater includes the less.' This may be a skilful evasion of the semantic problem but the intention is clear enough. There are aspects of religion which can be taught, and these must be well taught, but religion is a larger whole within which such instruction forms a limited but important part.

The early numbers of the journal contained articles which gave due emphasis to the whole and to the parts. The technical task of religious teaching was catered for in articles on the study of Israel's history, the study of the New Testament, syllabuses in secondary schools, problems in religious teaching and in an article by the editor on the opportunities available to teachers wishing to improve their professional equipment in this field. The larger issue was represented in some excellent general articles. There was also a thoughtful article by the Reverend Ronald Rees, then co-secretary of the National Council for Christian Religious Education in China, which illustrated very clearly the relationship between the parts and the whole.

Ronald Rees showed Christian educators, Chinese and foreign, asking searching questions about the nature and purpose of Christian education and deciding that it must not be limited to religious instruction. These Christian educators had become convinced by experience that the traditional substance of religious instruction 'was frequently quite unrelated to the real experience of growing boys and girls in China, their deepest needs and interests. A new kind of teaching was needed which would start there, meet the student on his own ground and transform not only his intellectual life but also his emotions, attitudes, habits and loyalties.'[3]

Educational missionaries from the U.S.A. had helped to carry the gospel of 'the new education' to China. Educational prophets like John Dewey and W. H. Kilpatrick had proclaimed the dawn of a new day. Pupils were not to be regarded as passive receptacles for knowledge whose interest in learning might be stimulated by skilful teaching techniques or by reward and punishment. Children were to be recognized as persons in their own right with interests and needs appropriate to their age. The teacher must provide a rich educational environment which would stimulate these interests and meet those needs. True growth comes from within and the whole growing person must be involved in it. Missionaries who had absorbed such ideas were able to interpret the failure and frustration of their Christian colleagues and to initiate a new policy in 'Christian religious education'. They were ready to recognize that Christian education, too, must provide for growth of the whole person.

This policy had been widely advocated in Christian missionary circles before the date of Ronald Rees's article. It was fully discussed at the Jerusalem meeting of the International Missionary Council in 1928 (*Religious Education*, Vol. II, Conference Report published by O.U.P.). It was described as educational evangelism (p. 59). It recognized the old truth that religion and education are each concerned with the whole of life. Christian education is a by-product of life within a Christian community. It happens as boys and girls grow up within such a community or as men and women are absorbed into the life of a Christian community. Formal education, with a Christian aim, must supplement these informal influences. Religious instruction should play a part, a limited but important part, within this larger whole. It should be integrated with it and it should be inseparable from it. The missionary educators were applying these truths to the specific needs of a missionary situation.

In that same period Christian educators were beginning to apply the same truths to religious education in this country. The term religious education was replacing the older term religious instruction, and the new term was obviously regarded as more inclusive in its implied aim. *The Cambridge Syllabus of Religious Teaching in Schools* (Revised edition 1939) gave prominence to an introductory article entitled 'Religion and Corporate Life in the School'. The article opened with the sentence: 'All education rightly conceived is religious education.' The opening paragraph contained the claim: 'So far therefore as the school is concerned, the initial question in religious education must be: Is the school a Christian community?'

The same insight influenced the thinking of those who planned, and those who implemented, the clauses governing compulsory religious education in the Education Act of 1944. The preliminary *White Paper on Educational Reconstruction* (1943) expressed their general intention: 'There has been a very general wish, not confined to representatives of the Churches, that religious education should be given a more defined place in the life and work of the schools, springing from the desire to revive the spiritual and personal values in our society and in our national tradition.' A sentence from the influential *London Syllabus of Religious Education*, published in 1947, shows how that intention found expression in the guidance offered to teachers. Introductory paragraphs on the use of the syllabus end with these sentences: 'Finally it is well to remember that the ultimate aim in religious education is not to get over to the child a body of facts – or "inert ideas", to use Professor Whitehead's phrase – but to inculcate and foster a comprehensible Way of Life. This Way of Life is summed up in the words of Our Lord: "Thou shalt love the Lord thy God with all thy heart, and with all thy soul, and with all thy mind . . . and thy neighbour as thyself."'

The intention could hardly be stated more clearly. Religious education should 'inculcate and foster' the Christian way of life. The intention is influenced by a valid insight. Religious education cannot be divorced from the total educational influence of the school. Religious instruction is only part of a larger whole. Religion and education are *both* concerned with the whole life of the growing child. Religious education is a false dichotomy.

The insight is incontrovertible but it had ceased to be relevant to the educational situation in Britain. It was not relevant when the 1944 Act was passed. The war-time mood of the country had disguised the real situation. It is much less relevant today. The words quoted from the London Syllabus have little meaning unless they are addressed by Christians to Christians. In a secularized society they have the hollow ring of pious platitudes. It is only possible to 'inculcate and foster a comprehensible way of life' in a community where belief and life are unified. A primitive society could inculcate and foster the tribal mores because these beliefs and customs were woven into the pattern of social life. A dynamic Christian, or communist, cell within an alien environment may foster its distinctive belief and life among its own members. The creative power of such a group may draw others into its membership. The state schools of a 'post-Christian society' are not, and cannot be, communities of this type. Human life may still have a religious dimension, but only a minority of the population interpret that dimension in traditional Christian terms.

Even church schools face a very difficult task in this secular age. The tension between traditional Christian teaching and contemporary culture is inescapable. The divorce between New Testament ethics and contemporary social and political life is blatantly obvious. The eager questioning mind and the loyal committed will seem to pull in opposite directions. Yet defensive dogmatism offers no lasting solution.

The missionary educators at the Jerusalem conference of 1928 had much to say about educational technique and training but these were not their supreme concern. They were convinced that the supreme need of their situation was 'a deeper religious experience, a new vital hold upon God, and a fresh grasp of the realities of life'. They called for a fresh dedication to 'a life of prayer and of trust in God and to new ventures in Christian living'.

The Christian church finds itself in a missionary situation today at home as well as abroad. Its problems will not be solved ultimately by new educational techniques. Its educational influence in its parochial and congregational activities, as well as in the schools under its control, depends on the creative power of its thought and life. Genuine Christian education awaits the emergence of a Christian community renewed and unified in thought and life.

Education with a Christian aim and intention may still be a possible ideal in church schools. It is not possible, even as an ideal, in the state schools of today and tomorrow. Can education still be religious in state schools? It has been argued that human life has a religious dimension and that that dimension has a vital place in personal development. What does this argument imply for education in state schools? Religious education is a misleading term. Religion and life belong together although traditional religion seems remote from contemporary life. Human life has an inescapable religious dimension and that dimension should be represented in the curriculum and life of the school. It should be integrated with the whole life of the school and it should find an appropriate place within the curriculum.

The meaning of such a statement must be examined in fuller detail later. The attitude which it implies may be clarified further by considering the change which has taken place in the title of the journal published by the Student Christian Movement Press. In September 1963 the 'terminal review' *Religion in Education* was replaced by a new journal with the title *Learning for Living*. The new title expressed a new approach. The gospel of 'the new education' was effecting a break-through at last in the strongholds of conservatism. Teachers must be encouraged 'to help their pupils towards critical choice and to see the aim of religious education in terms of personal search rather than the imparting of a body of facts'.[4] The new title, like the old one, recognized that the term *religious education* was inappropriate but it was more sensitive to current educational emphases. Learning must enrich living and it will only do so if the educational process is related to the pupils' needs and capacities.

The new title was expanded in a sub-title: *A Journal of Christian Education*. Here we meet the compromise and confusion which still bedevil Christian thinking about education. Christians might find no inconsistency between the title and the sub-title but non-Christians would surely raise awkward questions. Must 'learning for living' be done within the pattern of Christian belief and life? Is a truly 'open' approach really compatible with Christian education? An even more searching question might be raised from an opposite angle. Is 'learning for living' enough? The late Dr C. A. Alington was credited with the aphorism that education at Eton under his direction was 'for death'. Is this aim meaningful and important?

Perhaps the real aim of education is for living *and* for dying. 'Learning for Living' may be interpreted in a purely naturalistic sense. It may imply fostering the growth and enrichment of man's physical, mental and social capacities while ignoring man's deeper questionings. 'Why is there anything at all? Why is there not just nothing?' The philosopher's question is intellectually sophisticated but it points to that mystery which 'grazes' the consciousness of the human animal when he remembers his mortality. Learning for dying may be interpreted in a fully Christian sense – as Dr Alington doubtless intended. It may be governed by the belief that man is a creature of time whose life finds fulfilment in eternity. Christians would not accept the naturalistic aim. Humanists, agnostics and atheists would not accept the Christian aim. But all must acknowledge the fact of death and few, surely, would deny the significance of death for a right understanding of human life.

Is it possible to find a basis in such acknowledgment for a common educational policy? Is it possible to unite teachers in that 'passionate concern for truth which informed Socrates' saying that the unexamined life is not worth living' (see p. 38 above) – a passionate concern which refuses to ignore the ultimate mystery of death? Such a concern – were it shared consciously by teachers of many religious beliefs and of none – might restore a measure of unity and depth to our educational thinking and planning. It might begin to create the conditions for genuine wholeness in the educational curriculum. It might purge educational aims from class prejudice and political controversy and strengthen standards of excellence in all forms of educational enterprise. It might restore the religious dimension of human experience to its true central place in the thought and life of the school.

We can only begin to move in this direction if Christian educators recognize, more clearly than we have yet done, that Christian education cannot restore wholeness to the curriculum of state schools in the contemporary world. The Christian accepts, in the end, the 'risk of faith'. The non-Christian is unwilling to take that step. Christian aims do not offer a common goal for educational planning. Religious beliefs divide us. Recollection of our common humanity might unite us. We might unite in acknowledging the mystery which confronts us all and in exploring its educational implications.

8 Morality and Religion in Childhood

The English translation of Pierre Bovet's classic *Le Sentiment Religieux* (Delachaux et Niestlé, 1925, E.T.: *The Child's Religion*, London: Dent, 1928) has been out of print for many years. Its language and thought bear the mark of its period but its main argument still stands. It still provides a valuable way of approach to the study of morality and religion in childhood. Later developments in child psychology have deepened and clarified Bovet's original thesis.

Pierre Bovet and Jean Piaget were colleagues at the Jean Jacques Rousseau Institute in Geneva when Bovet's book was written and there are frequent references to Bovet's views on moral and religious development in Piaget's earlier writings. There are extensive quotations from Bovet in *The Moral Judgment of the Child* (London: Kegan Paul, 1932). In *The Child's Conception of the World* (London: Kegan Paul, 1929) Piaget supports his senior colleague's views on the origin of religion (see esp. p. 354 and pp. 377-386).

Piaget's own studies had convinced him that 'the child's real religion, at any rate during the first years, is quite definitely anything but the over-elaborated religion with which he is plied'.[1] Piaget endorsed Bovet's view that the child's 'real religion' originated in his relationship with his parents. The 'religious sentiment' originated in the 'filial sentiment'. In the terminology of the period a sentiment was 'an organized system of emotional tendencies centred about some object'.[2] The mother is all-important in the infant's earliest experience and, with the father, becomes the central object of the filial sentiment. Parents are the all-powerful, all-wise and perfect beings on whom the child's existence depends and to whom he becomes bound by complex emotional relationships of trust and love, fear and hate. The child 'spontaneously attributes to his parents the perfections and attributes which he will later transfer to God if his religious education gives him the opportunity'.[3]

Piaget claimed that traditional teaching in early years often appeared 'foreign to the child's natural thought'.[4] The child interprets the world around him in personal human terms. The material objects with which he is most familiar serve an obvious human purpose. A chair is 'for sitting on'. His mother uses it when she feeds or baths him. It is natural to assume that more remote and less familiar objects also serve human ends. The sun, the sea and the hills were also made 'for man'.

The transition from 'made for man' to 'made by man' is equally natural. New objects appear in the child's environment. The parents, or some other adult, produce them. Enquiry may reveal that they were brought from 'a shop'. 'A man' made them to serve the purposes of other men. When questions reach out beyond the immediate environment children fit the answers they receive into this anthropomorphic schema. These remote objects also serve human ends and so they must have been made by men for men. If children are told that God makes the sun, the sea and the hills they think of God as a very powerful man. They cannot do otherwise. God is still an 'unnecessary hypothesis'. The real religion of the child is taking shape within the 'filial sentiment'. His parents fill the divine role in his early experience.

Bovet and Piaget recognized that the filial sentiment began to change its character between the fourth and the seventh years of life. The limitations of the parents are becoming obvious. They do not know everything, they cannot do everything and they are not perfect. During these years the religious sentiment begins to develop from the filial sentiment. The moral experience 'I ought' emerges during this same period. It, too, has its roots in the filial sentiment but it is no longer identified solely with parental injunctions.[5] How do these changes take place? Bovet left this question unanswered but he showed that he recognized the depth and complexity of the problem. 'This problem,' he wrote, 'has never been sufficiently studied. It has scarcely even been propounded.'[6]

Ronald Goldman has made an important contribution to one aspect of this problem in *Religious Thinking from Childhood to Adolescence*. He makes considerable use of Piaget's series of influential volumes on different aspects of mental development and he also refers to Bovet's work. Goldman is concerned with 'the child's intellectual struggle to comprehend the central ideas expressed and implied in religious teaching'.[7] He has tried to find answers to such questions as: 'What is the nature of a child's religious thinking? How does he form concepts of God, of the Church, of moral rightness? Are there sequences or patterns of religious thought to be discerned with increasing chronological and mental age?'[8]

Goldman carried out a carefully prepared test with two hundred representative pupils between the ages of six and eighteen years. The test consisted of individual interviews and the average total length of the interview was one and a quarter hours. Each child was shown three pictures and listened to three Bible stories being played over on a tape recorder. Standardized questions were asked in each case and a measure of free discussion was allowed in the second part of the test. The stories selected were *Moses and the Burning Bush*, *Crossing the Red Sea* and *The Temptations of Jesus*. A simplified form of the biblical narrative was used in each case. The children's answers were carefully analysed and classified in relation to the ages of the children and conclusions were drawn which had disconcerting implications for traditional forms of religious teaching. Serious doubt was cast on the value of a Bible-based curriculum in the primary school.[9]

Goldman's conclusions have been hailed with enthusiasm in some quarters and severely criticized in others. It has been said, with some justice, that the questions put to the pupils were 'loaded' questions. They assumed a literal, traditional interpretation of the stories. Nevertheless his research has exposed a real problem. Religious experience uses the language of myth, symbol and metaphor. Primary school children interpret such language literally because their limited intellectual development makes it natural to do so. Biblical language and thought belong to an ancient world and an alien culture. They are perplexing for modern adults. How much more baffling must they seem to the minds of children.

Goldman maintains that intellectual understanding of religious imagery begins to be possible about the age of thirteen years. This claim seems to be soundly based. He is undoubtedly right in his general contention that syllabuses of religious teaching have tried to do 'too much too soon'. The criterion of 'readiness' is just as important in religious instruction as it is in arithmetic. But 'readiness for religion' must not be equated with readiness for intellectual understanding of religious concepts. Intellectual development is not the only criterion of religious readiness.

Goldman recognizes that 'emotional readiness' for religion pre-cedes intellectual readiness. The child needs security. When the limitations of parental care become obvious this need is transferred easily and naturally to the Heavenly Father.[10] There is a difficulty here, however, which Goldman does not discuss. When we intro-duce young children to religious language and religious practices we may be merely spreading a layer of conventional words and actions on the surface of their minds. We may not be fostering their real religious development.

John Macmurray reminded us in his Swarthmore lecture, *Search for Reality in Religion*, that 'Religion, however, and therefore religious development, is not primarily a matter of beliefs. The beliefs, so far as they are real, are derivative. The real religion from which they are derived lies in the depths of one's own being; its development is a development of one's personality itself.'[11] The 'real religion' of the child begins in the cradle. It is focused at first on the parents. They are 'the gods' of early childhood. When their power fails the focus of the child's religion begins to alter. Religious teaching may provide new 'gods' but it may not alter the set of the child's personal development. It may foster religiosity and fail to promote growth towards personal maturity. Primal trust and primal distrust have deeper roots and their relative influence on personal development is determined by more powerful factors.

What are those factors? How can we ensure a 'favourable ratio of trust over mistrust' (see p. 62 above) during the period of child-hood? Erik Erikson and other contemporary child psychologists agree with Bovet in stressing the significance of the parent-child relationship in the earliest years of life. Bovet was concerned specifically with the religious significance of that relationship but he discussed it in psychological terms. He was a Christian believer but, as a psychologist, he disclaimed any responsibility for deciding whether 'it is reasoned fear or instinctive confidence which will penetrate more deeply into the mystery of the universe'.[12] Con-temporary psychologists are concerned primarily with the psycho-logical significance of the parent-child relationship, but they discuss it in ways which have obvious religious implications.

Brief reference has already been made to Erikson's discussion of basic trust and basic mistrust (see chapter 6 above). The whole subject is highly technical and controversial but certain common factors are widely supported in current psychological literature. One of these may be illustrated by a short quotation from Melanie Klein's pamphlet *Our Adult World and its Roots in Infancy*:

The young infant, without being able to grasp it intellectually, feels unconsciously every discomfort as though it were inflicted on him by hostile forces. If comfort is given to him soon – in particular warmth, the loving way he is held, and the gratification of being fed – this gives rise to happier emotions. Such comfort is felt to come from good forces and, I believe, makes possible the infant's first loving relation to a person.[13]

The title of Melanie Klein's pamphlet is significant. The development of psychology since Bovet's day has emphasized the importance of the 'filial sentiment'. The child's earliest experiences of the world into which he has been born come through personal relationships, and the quality of these relationships has a profound influence on the strains and tensions of adult life. In these early relationships the child is forming his first attitudes towards the unknown world into which he has come. The experience of love awakens trust and creates the possibility of loving relationships with other persons. The relationship with 'the gods' of infancy helps to determine the child's later relationships with 'the gods' of maturity and with his fellow human beings.

Separation from the mother is widely recognized as a significant factor in child development. John Bowlby has reported results of extensive investigations on this topic. These studies were carried out in this country and abroad. They included studies of young apes as well as of human infants between one and three years of age. The young apes showed a strong tendency to cling physically to the mother. They showed evidence of disturbed behaviour, as human infants also did, when they were separated from the mother. Bowlby reached the conclusion that separation from the mother touches depths in human nature which belong to our biological inheritance.[14]

The significance of 'separation anxiety' is interpreted in a fresh way by the American psychologist Adah Maurer in an article entitled 'Maturation of Concepts of Death'. Maurer recognizes in this anxiety a deep inner awareness of a threat to life itself: 'At some level below true cognition, the child with naive narcissism "knows" that the loss of his parents is the loss of his tie to life. Left alone with strangers or in a strange place he feels abandoned without hope of rescue. Total terror for his life rather than jealous possessiveness of a chosen and lost love object is the aetiology of the somatic distress of separation anxiety.'[15]

Maurer traces this 'awareness' of a threat to existence back to the very beginnings of the child's personal development. The new-born infant begins slowly to distinguish between 'self' and 'not-self'. The first wavering emergence of an 'ego' becomes evident as he differentiates himself from his environment.'But the true opposite of a sense of being is a sense of non-being. The baby comes to have a sense of these two states as he wavers back and forth over the threshold of consciousness alternating between wakefulness and sleep. The transition is not always easy as anyone who has tried to put a baby to sleep or listened to him cry himself to sleep will testify. Awakening, too, is sometimes piecemeal. Uneven restoration of the circulation of the brain, perhaps, or some other incomplete physiological signals sometimes give rise to a frightening half-here feeling. When the infant, whose hold on consciousness is somewhat tenuous, wakens in the dark of a quiet house, deprived of signals from two senses and perhaps more, he is gripped by this sensation of disembodiment and lets go with the unearthly shriek that doctors call "night terrors".'[16]

This interpretation is speculative and controversial but it is also thought-provoking and pertinent to our argument. Maurer emphasizes the importance of death for personal development. His argument illuminates Heidegger's analysis and supports the conclusion that development from infancy to maturity is profoundly influenced by human awareness of finitude. The threat of 'non-being' is a vital factor in that 'ratio of primal trust and primal distrust' which shapes personal development. Maurer describes awareness of being and non-being as 'the first of the series of adaptations to the fact of a finite life. It remains always the inner core of what will be a man who loves life and knows its negation.'[17] Religion begins in this awareness of finitude. 'Without this knowledge of death, I came to believe, there can be no real knowledge of life and so no discovery of the reality of religion.'[18]

Piaget and Bovet believed that the religious dimension of human need is satisfied in early years by the loving care of parents. Subsequent developments in psychology have added depth and complexity to that truth. Bovet described a 'first religious crisis' associated with the child's discovery of parental limitations. Maurer describes a pre-cognitive 'awareness' of non-being. This awareness breaks the surface of consciousness when the first 'gods' fail. At this point the ultimate loneliness of human existence touches the child's life. Bovet placed this 'crisis' around the sixth year of life. There are wide individual variations in personal development but the norm should probably be placed earlier. It may be linked with the three to five year period which Freudians call the oedipus phase in personal development.

This is a time of growing personal awareness. The ego is becoming consolidated as a relatively stable expression of the individual's habitual responses to his environment. The super-ego has developed as an inner mechanism controlling behaviour – conscience as we call it normally. Erikson names initiative and guilt as the two poles between which human experience and human behaviour oscillate at this stage of development. The child is moving beyond the initial stage of dependence on the adult world. Personal initiative is developing. The measure of trust and mistrust which characterized the child's early experiences affects his relative success or failure at this stage. The child who has learned to trust can enter on a more independent life with freedom and confidence. His relationships with other children, with the adult world, with new tasks and responsibilities are relatively unhampered by inner fears and tensions. The mistrustful child tends to withdraw from the tasks and responsibilities of the real world. The development of authentic and inauthentic ways of living can be traced back to the beginning of conscious existence. The choice between the two ways has special difficulties and hazards at this stage.

Erikson tells the story of a boy of three years of age who developed a series of perplexing attacks of an epileptic character. He came to Erikson as a patient two years after the first attack and his treatment lasted for some time. The child's first three major attacks were all connected with ideas of death. Two later ones were associated with the successive disappearance of two persons who had been playing an important and intimate part in his life. They occurred when a new therapist replaced one who had grown familiar.

It would be easy to isolate one factor in this boy's story and to over-emphasize the importance which experience of death has at this stage of child development. This would be seriously misleading. Erikson's account of this case is most instructive. It shows very clearly the complexity of personal development. Erikson draws attention to constitutional factors, social factors and developmental factors. There was some evidence of cerebral irritability. The boy belonged to a Jewish family living in a Gentile environment and he shared its traditions and social tensions. He had reached a period of special difficulty in personal development. A grandmother's death may have been a precipitating psychic factor but it was only one of a complex series of circumstances. 'Of the "catastrophe" . . . we know no "cause". Instead we find a convergence . . . which makes the catastrophe retrospectively intelligible, retrospectively probable.'[19]

The 'religious dimension' of life cannot be isolated from the complexity of human experience. 'Primal trust and primal mistrust' enter into every experience and influence every stage of personal development. The ratio of trust and mistrust is influenced in turn by the experiences of each stage of life. In early childhood such trust and distrust is focused on the parents. In the period between the fourth and sixth year of life the focus changes. The child becomes aware of a basic insecurity in human existence which the parents cannot control.

Evidence of anxiety about death finds frequent expression at this stage in emotional disturbance and in questions tinged with anxiety. Violet Madge describes a typical conversation between a mother and a child of four and a half years:

Child   Mummy, what means a dead mother?
Mother A woman that has died and does not walk or talk any more.
Child   But what will the children do?
Mother Well, if a mother should die, the father would take care of them and maybe an aunt.
Child   Will you be a dead mother some day?
Mother Why yes, though I don't expect to be for a long time.
Child   A *very* long time?
Mother Yes.
Child   But I don't want you to die; I want you here like this.
Mother Well you will probably be quite grown up before that happens.
Child   A *long* time.
Mother Yes.
Child   But what *means* dead, mummy.
Mother Well, your heart stops beating and you lie still without breathing.
Child   And what do you do with the talking part – you know the inside talk?

Mother I'm not sure, but some people think you live in another world, and, of course, some don't.

Child I guess we do (excitedly). Yes! And then you die in a *long*, long time – a *very* long time, and I die and we both hug each other and then you won't have any wrinkles – Oh, look at that cute pussy. Isn't she darling? (Runs off.)[20]

This story is typical of the anxiety about death which shows itself frequently in spontaneous questions at the pre-school stage. The closing point of the conversation draws attention to the child's real need at this stage. The verbal answers to his questions are relatively unimportant. They were largely ignored. Intellectual readiness for religion still lies far ahead. The child needs emotional reassurance and will find it, or fail to find it, at the deeper levels of his nature in the measure of serenity with which the adult world accepts this disturbing new fact in his experience. At the conscious level he may tend to deny the reality of death. One contemporary writer tells that children between the ages of four and seven whom she questioned 'showed a firm determination to believe that death does not happen, that it is not irreversible, that some people escape, that there are various degrees of death, or that it can be avoided by good behaviour'.[21]

Individual children will find their several ways of dealing with this new and disturbing experience. Its significance in their personal development cannot be isolated from the complex constitutional, social and personal factors which have already influenced that development. It is a fresh psychic stimulus which calls for a new step in personal response. The basic attitudes of his parents, of the adult world around him, can help to strengthen the child's basic trust in face of this new threat to his security. The new unknown 'gods' are more likely to be trusted if children find trust expressed in those deeper levels of parental attitude which speak more loudly than words.

The religious dimension of life tends to drop into the background of consciousness during the later years of childhood. Spontaneous questions of a religious character do not cease abruptly at the age of five years. Questions tinged with anxiety can occur at any stage throughout the primary school. The anxiety may figure in dreams or it may touch waking hours without finding verbal expression. When it appears above the surface of life at home, or at school, it is commonly associated with some disturbing emotional experience. The child's relationship to 'the gods' does not normally figure explicitly during this period.

Violet Madge's study of scientific and religious interests in primary school children helps to confirm this view. In her book she tells that she found few specifically religious interests among the spontaneous questions asked by pupils of five to seven years. Those which did appear seemed to reflect intellectual perplexity arising from contact with adult teaching and practice: 'If Jesus was God who made Mary?' 'How can God possibly make room in heaven for everyone for ever and ever?'[22] Such questions were typical. They raise important issues for religious teaching at that stage but they do not suggest any spontaneous interest in religious questions. The religious dimension is still implicit in the whole of life but it seldom touches consciousness.

Violet Madge has some interesting comments on the spontaneous feelings of wonder and awe which appear in primary-school pupils – especially in the younger classes. These feelings were associated especially, she tells us, with the wonders of the natural world, with awareness of the frontiers of human knowledge, with birth and death and with human relationships. Such moments of mystery occur more readily in the freedom of a modern school class room. They are only likely to be expressed in the presence of sympathetic, sensitive and perceptive teachers and parents. They are important growing points of the human spirit and they have a natural affinity with worship.

The stage between the seventh and the twelfth year of life is important socially. Children are learning a multitude of skills in work and in play which bring them into close relationship with their fellows. They are beginning to acquire the confidence which achieve-ment brings. They are threatened by feelings of inferiority due to failure. Such feelings of confidence or inferiority are influenced by, and react upon, the primal attitudes of trust and distrust. Each child's complex pattern of typical social behaviour is being woven by individual responses to a series of changing experiences.

The school has a very important part to play in moral education at this stage. The pressures of social tradition and wise social discipline may help to develop a pattern of social behaviour which satisfies children's inner needs and is socially acceptable. Such pressures will not cure the inner tensions and fears from which anti-social behaviour springs. The healing influences of love are needed to reduce these tensions and to cast out these fears.

At this point the religious dimension of life is again relevant. The love which can heal is not a sentimental 'love' which is an outlet for unsatisfied needs in parents or teacher. It is love of the type described in the New Testament. Such love has its roots in the adult's relationship to the ultimate mysteries of human existence. The supreme task of the adult towards the younger generation and towards the immature of all ages is to provide this healing love. This is the heart of moral and religious education at every stage. Only the mature can help the immature. 'Healthy children will not fear life if their elders have integrity enough not to fear death.'[23]

9 The Religious Dimension in Primary Education

The transition from home to school is an important stage in personal development. It occurs at a time when children are just emerging from the security of parental care. They have lost their first 'gods' and they are taking their early steps towards independent personal living. Circumstances vary greatly according to home circumstances and social background. A nursery school, a day nursery, or some baby-minding establishment may have begun the weaning process before the normal age for school entry. The first days at school may be emotionally disturbing for some children. They are emotionally important for all children. They are learning to live in a wider world with new patterns of acceptable behaviour and new impersonal relationships. They must face new fears and master new skills.

Throughout all these experiences the basic attitudes of trust and distrust are being modified and the relative balance is being affected. Children are learning to face the uncertainties and insecurities of life trustfully and courageously or they are developing feelings of distrust and attitudes of defensive withdrawal or aggression. Moral and religious education cannot be isolated from the total pattern of class room life. Adult insight, sympathy and disinterested concern are the media through which personal development is fostered. They are the most important media of moral and religious education in the early years of the primary school.

The early balance of trust and mistrust is already established before pupils enter the primary school. Individual responses to the diverse experiences of early years have made some children trustful, free and courageous while others are inwardly insecure and outwardly defensive and ego-centric. These basic attitudes will affect their class-room behaviour and their relationships with their fellow-pupils. The perceptive teacher will be aware of the outer difficulties and sensitive to the inner needs. The smaller classes and the freer methods of modern schools make it easier for teachers to deal with the difficulties of individual children, to consult with parents and, where desirable, to seek specialist assistance. This, too, is moral and religious education.

Susan Isaacs' familiar concept of the 'good-strict' mother[1] is still a helpful guide for primary-school teachers as well as for parents. Young children need the assurance of an orderly class-room life where personal freedom and activity is encouraged by love and supported by firm but flexible control. In such a class-room children can learn to be trustful in their dealings with one another. They can learn to be trustworthy through class-room traditions of honesty, reliability and fair-play. They can learn to care for others and to be helpful to others in the class-room community and in wider areas of human need.

Many children will have been exposed to religious teaching in the home or the Sunday School. Religious ideas and practices will be woven into the fabric of their basic attitudes. They will be important emotionally for some but not for others. They would be reflected at times in pupils' spontaneous comments and questions even if religion had no explicit place in school life. How should teachers deal with such questions and comments? Much must depend on the teacher's own attitude and convictions but dogmatic answers may tend to close doors in the mind which should be opening to the wonders of the world. The Christian teacher may find it natural to speak of the wonders of *God's* world but children from homes where religious belief is conventional or non-existent will have no inner experience which might interpret that word. The word *God* may be little more than an intellectual puzzle for such children.

Knowledge and experience brings us all to the frontiers of genuine mystery. Children reach these frontiers more quickly because their knowledge and experience is so limited. Wonder is awakened frequently and naturally. Moments of wonder should be fostered and enriched by more knowledge and wider experience. They may be dulled by premature use of religious explanations. The words 'God did it' may stifle genuine thought and feeling. They may substitute the false mystery which is born of ignorance and begets superstition for the true mystery which lies beyond the frontiers of all knowledge.

Young children become familiar with many words which they do not understand. Parents and teachers do not avoid using the word electricity because it cannot be explained satisfactorily to young children. If they are asked to explain such words children give answers which are just as fortuitous and fantastic as their efforts to interpret religious language. Piaget gives a brief extract from a conversation which shows a child of nine and a half years wrestling with the word electricity.

'How did the sun begin? – *I don't know, it's not possible to say.* – You are right there, but we can guess. Has there always been a sun? – *No. It's the electricity which has always been growing more and more.* – Where does this electricity come from? – *From under the earth, from water.* – What is electricity? – *It's the current.* Can a current of water make electricity? – *Yes.* – What is this current made of? – *It's made of steam.*' (Steam, electricity and current seem to him to be all the same thing.) 'How did the electricity make the sun? – *It is current which has escaped.* – How has it grown? – *It's the air which has stretched, the electricity has been made bigger by the air.*'[2]

Such confused irrational talk about electricity raises no educational problem. We know that the same child will discuss the same themes in a logical, rational way at a later stage of intellectual development. He must reach the stage of 'readiness for physics' before he can be expected to talk meaningfully about electricity. We do not attempt to teach physics to young children but we do not refrain from introducing the word electricity into their vocabulary. Should we be any more hesitant about premature use of religious concepts?

The parallel is instructive. Young children talk meaningless nonsense if they are asked to explain the word electricity but the word itself is meaningful to them at the level of action. They cannot talk about the nature of electricity but they know what electricity does. Electricity is 'for cooking', 'for heating', 'for helping us to see in the dark' and so on. But what about *God*? If we teach children to look for God's action in the world of nature we may create intellectual puzzles and close their minds to the genuine mystery which hides the nature of God from the mind of man. 'Behold God is great and we know him not' (Job 36.26).

God may often 'hide himself' in the world of nature and of

history but he makes himself known in the inner life and outer action of those who truly seek him and who respond to the leading of his spirit. When God is real to parents the word God is meaningful to their children. They cannot talk about God rationally but they begin to understand the word at the level of human experience. Children are sensitive to feeling and emotion and they are conscious of changing human attitudes. Genuine religious feeling which finds expression in human action speaks at a deeper level than words. Genuine adult worship may begin to interpret religious concepts long before children are 'ready for religion' intellectually. The attitudes and actions of 'the gods' who have been dethroned direct them towards the God above 'the gods'.[3]

The real educational difficulty arises with pupils – and they are many – who have no such experience in their early years. They lack any inner reality which can grow in depth and meaning. Religious concepts can only be interpreted crudely and concretely. When such interpretations break down nothing remains and religion is liable to be dismissed as childish nonsense. Ronald Goldman attempts to deal with this difficulty by using 'life-themes' as a central element in his 'developmental' curriculum. He seeks to make religious imagery meaningful by enlarging children's experience and deepening their understanding of biblical metaphors. His 'life-themes' have admirable features but they have one serious defect.

This defect can be illustrated from the theme called *The Importance of Bread* which he discusses in *Readiness for Religion*. It is planned for pupils of seven to eight years. Ten work cards are provided for pupils' use. The individual titles of these cards give some impression of their intention:

> The food we like and the food we need.
> What goes into bread?
> Flour from wheat.
> Growing the wheat.
> The wonder of wheat.
> Making our own bread.
> Making bread in Jesus' home.
> A modern bakery.
> Bread for the world.
> Special occasions.[4]

Goldman makes this comment on the purpose of these cards:

They [children] see bread, they eat it, but most children these days have little insight into its real nature or its significance for daily life. Again, there are many rich religious metaphors which are lost, simply because experience is limited and children need to explore in depth, the experience of bread which they already have, if they are to recognize its centrality and to apprehend its religious significance. By making bread, seeing its elements, watching yeast working, and discovering for themselves the mysterious process of breadmaking, we are putting real life experience alongside religious truth, so that knowing ordinary life at depth becomes a religious experience.[5]

Goldman's justification for this last statement does not rest on any spontaneous experience of the pupils. It rests on the use of religious language and religious suggestion in the wording of the cards. The last card in the series contains these sentences:

Another Special Occasion

The time when Jesus lived on earth sometimes seems very long ago . . . But there are some things which can bring the days of Jesus and our days very close together. One of these is bread.
This is why:

The Last Supper

Jesus had supper with his disciples on the last night before he died. During supper he passed round bread and wine to them, which had a special meaning. This is what the Bible says about it:
  'During supper he took bread and having said the blessing he broke it and gave it to them, with the words: "Take this, this is my body." '
In churches ever since then, however differently they do it, groups of Christians have gone to worship God and meet each other to break bread, to think about Jesus and to pray. This is still done today. What can you find out about it?

Something to Remember

Jesus said that everyone who is hungry for what is good, shall be satisfied.[6]

This is not pupil-centred education. This is adult indoctrination. These closing words introduce religious language which is still far beyond the understanding of eight-year-old children. The idea of being 'hungry for what is good' cannot be made meaningful in this way. The first steps towards understanding such a concept do not depend primarily on a fuller imaginative understanding of the importance of bread. They depend on children's contact with that quality in human living. The real task of the state school is to enrich pupils' inner experience in ways which may awaken religious feeling and provide a pre-cognitive core of meaning which may gradually interpret religious language. This brings us at once to the theme of worship in the primary school.

In early years worship will naturally be informal. It must be adapted to local circumstances and to the outlook and attitude of the teacher. Class-room worship should not involve teachers in conscious insincerity but perceptive teachers may be able to use moments of spontaneous wonder as growing points in the experience of genuine worship. Violet Madge makes many helpful comments on this subject in her book *Children in Search of Meaning*. 'Such wonder,' she writes, '. . . was evident in Sally's puzzled amazement when she caused iron filings to move by using a magnet, and exclaimed: "Look, they're wriggling, they're wriggling." '[7] Commenting on such experience she writes: 'From this elemental sense of the mysterious moments of wonder akin to worship seem occasionally to arise . . . They may well possess more of the true essence of worship than the usual adult-directed form, in so far as the younger children are concerned.'[8]

As children grow older myths and stories from many lands and cultures might be used in association with worship. The great myths of mankind may speak to deeper levels of the developing personality before the mind is able to understand religious concepts. The Epic of Gilgamish contains material which could be used along with the biblical stories of creation and the flood. Such juxtaposition would help to lift the biblical myths out of the category of literal history. It would set them free to speak directly to the levels of feeling and emotion. Musical and dramatic techniques might be used in connection with such myths.

Many stories from the Old and New Testaments might speak in this same way. The stories of Moses at the Bush and of the call of Isaiah create difficulties in religious teaching because irrelevant questions about historicity and literal interpretation destroy their 'numinous' quality. The first of these stories can be used with younger primary classes and the second with older pupils if these irrelevant issues can be avoided. Such stories appeared in 'progressive' syllabuses forty years ago under headings like 'Stories told to Jesus' but few teachers accepted the freedom offered by these words. The limitations of the teachers defeated the intention of the syllabus compilers.

The devil of literalism might be exorcised more successfully if selections from other great religious traditions were included among stories used in the primary school. Even the *Crossing of the Red Sea* might claim a place as a Hebrew 'wonder story' and the 'pillar of cloud and fire' might regain its former power. Such stories should not be taught as part of biblical 'history' and they should not be used for direct religious teaching. They belong to the religious traditions of mankind and they may speak, as stories from non-biblical traditions may also speak, to levels of feeling and emotion which abstract language cannot touch. 'The conquest of literalism without loss of the symbols is the great task for religious education.'[9]

Similar principles should guide the handling of the 'miraculous' elements from the New Testament in the state primary schools. The nativity stories will naturally figure in primary-school teaching. Some Christians would wish to retain the traditional 'supernatural' character of these stories and would regard the miraculous happenings as God's witness to the birth of his Son. Non-Christians, and many Christians, would think of them as the Early Church's witness to its belief about the nature of Jesus. The former view may have its place in Christian teaching. It is not appropriate in the state school setting. Christians differ in the degree of historicity which they find in these stories. All teachers would surely agree that such stories are akin to poetry in their educational value. The clue to their appropriate treatment lies in that fact. When these stories are treated as literal history they raise puzzles for the mind. Primary school pupils know, for instance, that no star could guide men to a house unless it came down out of the sky and hovered directly over the house. When teachers attempt to 'historicize' such a story they are forced to introduce details which are not in the original narrative. In doing so they destroy the simple poetic beauty of the story and they may cause unnecessary perplexity.

The gospel miracles and the resurrection narratives present similar problems. The same principles should govern the teacher's approach to them. Christians differ here also but all teachers may find common ground in acknowledging that these narratives, in their present form at least, are evidence of the church's faith. They were intended to strengthen and inform the faith of the church and to bear witness to Christian belief about Jesus of Nazareth. That belief cannot be assumed as a basis for teaching in state primary schools but primary schools should be introduced to stories appropriate to their age as part of early Christian tradition about Jesus. It would be inappropriate to stress the wonder element in these stories. It would be equally inappropriate to rationalize them. They should be told simply and directly. Historical and geographical detail should be introduced freely. Jesus of Nazareth was a historical figure and he can only be understood in his historical setting. The emphasis should be on Jesus's concern for others and no attempt should be made to 'historicize' the 'supernatural' element or to explain it away. Stories from the life of Gautama Buddha, or other similar figures of religious traditions, might be introduced to show that legendary and didactic elements are present in all religious traditions. Suitable material from other traditions may be sparse but it should not be omitted. Older pupils might be introduced to some of the legendary tales from the apocryphal gospels.

Verbal teaching in the primary school should be factual and preparatory, rather than directly religious in intention. It should be focused on the person of Jesus. Primary pupils in state schools should learn that 'Jesus of Nazareth taught men to trust God's love and to show love to others'. The teaching should show Jesus in his contemporary Jewish setting. It should provide factual teaching which may prepare pupils to understand, in later years, the meaning of the original Christian claim 'Jesus is the Messiah'.

Such teaching should include facts about the Jewish faith in which Jesus was nurtured and about the social, political and religious setting of his early life. This information can be conveyed in simple, concrete ways. Pupils might learn the words of the *Shema* and become familiar with the Jewish use of the *mezuzah*. They might learn about such Jewish feasts as the sabbath, the feast of lights and the feast of the passover. The passover question 'Why is this night different from all other nights?' would focus attention on Jewish belief in a God-given vocation associated with an experience of deliverance. The 'cup for Elijah' at the passover supper would be a concrete illustration of the Jewish hope. Stories of the fishermen, the Pharisees, the tax-collectors and the Roman soldiers whom Jesus met could be used to introduce pupils to the social circumstances, the troubles and the hopes of first-century Jews.

In older classes it would be appropriate to include stories of men and women in later centuries, and in modern times, who have followed Jesus's way of love in creative social and personal action. Men and women from many lands and from other races should be included. Such story material should not be confined to Christians but should include other great figures from the moral and spiritual history of mankind.

Old Testament material can be introduced in association with Jewish festivals. Stories of Moses, David and Elijah can be used in this context. These Old Testament figures belong to the pattern of Jewish belief and provide links with the New Testament. The words *vocation, failure* and *hope* provide a simple clue to the pattern of biblical belief. Moses brought the Israelites out of Egypt, led them into covenant with God and gave them God's law. Jewish belief in a God-given *vocation* is based on this experience of deliverance from slavery. Elijah was typical, in Jewish tradition, of the prophets who accused their people of *failure* in their vocation. Jews believed that he would come again to prepare their people for God's perfect age (cf. Mal. 4.5). Jewish memories of David's reign coloured their *hope* of a 'son of David' who would be God's Messiah. Such beliefs can be introduced in concrete ways by association with Jewish practices. This can provide a valuable preparation for secondary-school teaching and can help to put the historical narratives in the context of Jewish belief. Older pupils should be helped to recognize that historical fact and Jewish belief are intermingled in the historical narratives (cf. II Kings 17.6f.). They should realize what varied types of literature are contained in the Old Testament and how many centuries of history are reflected on its pages. They should begin to see the New Testament as the writings of a Jewish sect who were convinced that the purpose of God had been fulfilled and that Jesus of Nazareth was the expected Messiah.

Story material will always have a place in the primary school and the art of the storyteller will always be a valuable asset in younger classes but modern primary methods recognize the importance of pupil activity in learning. This modern emphasis breaks down the barrier between 'subjects'. The many-sided 'project' is replacing the traditional subjects. The formal element cannot be eliminated from primary education but it should not be allowed to hamper the natural growth and expression of spontaneous interests.

Most of the material described in the previous paragraphs can be adapted readily to modern practice. Old Testament material from the period of Solomon might be used in top primary classes as a basis for group activities which cross many subject frontiers. Selected passages from I Kings might be read in order to find out about trading routes, about the variety of goods taken into Palestine and exported from Palestine, about Solomon's building activities, where building material came from and how it was paid for. Three groups could work on these three main themes and report on their discoveries. Models and maps could be prepared and included in the reports presented by the groups. Reference books would help the pupils to interpret the passages given them for study and to enlarge their knowledge of the social and industrial development during this period. The whole enterprise could be used to throw light on the reasons for the abortive revolt during Solomon's reign and for the division in the kingdom after Solomon's death. The biblical narratives would be used to illustrate the contrast between Solomon's regal tyranny and the prophetic ideals of Hebrew kingship (cf. Deut. 17.14-20). Solomon was remembered in Jewish tradition as a man of wide culture and great achievement but it was David who coloured Jewish hopes for the future.

Goldman's 'life-themes' are an admirable educational device for integrating religious teaching with other elements in the primary school curriculum in ways which utilize pupils' interests and engage their activities. Their weakness lies in their aims and intentions. Goldman seems to think that Christian education is still the ultimate objective of religious teaching in state schools. There are curious inconsistencies in his position. In *Readiness for Religion* he claims that 'Religion is eminently a personal search, a personal experience and a personal challenge'.[10] On later pages he makes other claims. He states that 'The Christian faith is a frame of reference through which everything can be experienced, related and interpreted'.[11] He also writes: 'The unifying principle, spoken by the teacher, or to be assumed by the child, is that all we learn about the world is a knowledge of God's world, of his creation and his power.'[12]

Goldman seems to ignore three important facts. The first is that 'personal search' will not necessarily lead to an acceptance of the Christian faith. The second is that many teachers in state schools would not accept the Christian faith as a 'unifying principle' in all learning. The third fact is that large numbers of boys and girls in state schools today have no experience of Christian belief and practice at home which might provide some inner understanding of concepts which are beyond their intellectual grasp. Many of Goldman's suggestions might be very fruitful within a believing community. The aims and intentions of his life-themes are hardly relevant to the problems of the state school.

Goldman seems strangely unwilling to recognize the implications of his own investigations. The use of the Bible for direct religious teaching in state primary schools has very severe limitations in an age which cannot accept pre-critical literalism. Biblical imagery, the alien idiom of biblical thought, the many layers of moral and religious insight within the pages of the Bible make it an impossible text-book for direct moral and religious teaching in the primary school. But the Old Testament contains essential material for understanding the faith of Israel in which Christian belief and life had their roots. Factual teaching which prepares for such later understanding is the appropriate contribution of the primary school to the Christian element in religious teaching. The living faith of Israel provides a focus for concrete factual teaching. Similar teaching from the New Testament finds a natural focus in the words and deeds of Jesus of Nazareth whom some Jews recognized as their Messiah. The essential methods of the life theme can be adapted to such factual teaching although the aims and intentions would be different.

A programme of religious education for primary classes in state schools should accept two main objectives. It should seek to foster and deepen the awareness of mystery which touches the experience of young children at so many points. Violet Madge refers helpfully to this dimension of mystery in her book. She finds it associated with the wonders of the natural world, awareness of the frontiers of human knowledge, with birth and death and with human relationships. The sensitive and perceptive primary school teacher will find many opportunities for fostering such experiences of 'natural religion'.

What about 'revealed religion'? What place remains for Christian teaching? An objective approach to Christian origins might be acceptable to Christian and non-Christian alike as an element within the secondary-school curriculum. A completely objective approach is hardly feasible in the primary school. Logical consistency is impossible in the present confused situation. Circumstances and attitudes differ greatly from region to region and from school to school. Neither pupils nor teachers can separate themselves from the social and religious influences around them. These influences – as they touch the primary school child – are still strongly coloured by Christian belief and practice. Traditional beliefs will colour the approach of many teachers. It will colour the thinking of many pupils. Complete consistency is impossible.

A clear declaration of objective intent is desirable, however, if Christian and non-Christian teachers are to co-operate in a common policy. Goldman's conclusions suggest that we should not press direct religious teaching on young children. They are not ready for it intellectually. It is not meaningful for them emotionally unless they come from Christian homes. We should be content to limit our verbal teaching to such factual knowledge as may prepare pupils for a later understanding of the source and meaning of Christian love. This would seem to imply factual teaching about Jesus of Nazareth from whom men have learned how to live, in whom men have seen perfect love. Such factual teaching may prepare for the adolescent stage when pupils must find new 'gods' to replace the parental image and the parental law of early childhood.

10 Morality and Religion in Adolescence

A new and important phrase in personal development begins as adolescence approaches. It is a particularly difficult phase in contemporary social life. Erikson tells us that the psychiatric 'patient of today suffers most under the problem of what he should believe in and who he should – or, indeed, might – be or become'.[1] The psychiatrist in his consulting room meets those who have broken down under the stress of personal tensions and social pressures. His patients are not typical of their generation. Yet the problems of the abnormal may throw light on the inner strains and the outer behaviour of their normal contemporaries.

The problem of 'ego-identity', as it is called nowadays, is not a new one. The problem belongs to the dynamics of personal development in all ages from the first emergence of self-awareness in mankind. The young child develops an ego in early childhood. He develops an habitual pattern of responses to the social pressures that play upon him. This ego is a more or less stable compromise between inner needs and outer pressures. In happy circumstances the ego formation is reasonably well integrated with the unconscious layers of the personality. The individual is well adapted to the real world. In less happy circumstances the ego is a protective shield behind which the inner forces of the personality take refuge from the real world and its demands. In such circumstances inner pressures tend to show themselves in aggressive or submissive behaviour. The ego structure must be maintained. Behaviour becomes unduly 'egocentric'. In most circumstances the ego formation adopted in early childhood remains relatively stable throughout the primary school stage. At that stage most children are predictable creatures. We know, more or less, how different individuals are likely to behave in normal circumstances.

The ego-formation of early childhood involves individual responses. The early compromise between inner needs and social pressures depends on individual characteristics. Each individual develops his own characteristic style of life during these early years. It is an *individual* achievement but it is not yet a fully *personal* achievement. Ego-identity becomes a *personal* problem in adolescence. Full personal freedom is still a distant goal but the burden of conscious decision is now awaiting acceptance. The infant is thrust out from the mother's womb to begin an independent physical existence. The adolescent is thrust out from the shelter of adult care to begin an independent personal existence. He must win economic independence. He must enter into personal relationships with his fellow men and find his appropriate place among them. New emotional urges will find their appropriate satisfaction in mating and in parenthood. The ultimate loneliness and mystery of human existence may 'graze' his consciousness in moments of spiritual awareness.

The infant's transition from life in the womb to independent physical existence is eased by maternal nurture. The infant must be weaned gradually from the complete physical dependence of the early days. The adolescent, too, needs social support in achieving personal independence. Psychological weaning is even more hazardous and difficult than physical weaning. Unresolved strains and tensions from early years re-emerge with new strength. The individual compromise between inner needs and outer pressures may be endangered. It must certainly be modified and adapted to express a *personal* style of life.

In primitive communities initiation rites provided a social device for ensuring individual conformity to the normal pattern of adult behaviour. Each new generation was initiated into the adult mores. Adolescents learned what they should believe and how they should act in the three basic areas of adult life, in their relationships with the opposite sex, in their social functions and responsibilities and in their relationship with the gods – those unknown mysterious powers who controlled the forces of nature and the destinies of men. This adolescent learning was done under conditions of emotional pressure which are paralleled in the more sophisticated modern techniques of brain-washing. Non-conformists, social deviants, 'rogue elephants' appeared in the most primitive forms of human – and even sub-human – society but they were few. The adolescent problem of ego-identity hardly existed at that stage of social development.

During two thousand years of Christian history there have been periods of relative stability in western society when social pressures served a function parallel to that of initiation rites. Late nineteenth-century Britain is an illustration. Of course there were many 'sub-cultures' within Victorian England and Scotland. There was hypocrisy. There were turbulent tides of change already breaking the placid surface of Victorian tradition. Yet there was a general pattern of belief and behaviour which provided an acceptable social norm. The couplet,

> God bless the squire and his relations
> And help us keep our proper stations,

is not entirely a caricature of Victorian English piety. It finds support in that part of the Anglican catechism where the question occurs: 'What is thy duty towards thy neighbour?' The reply includes these phrases: 'To order myself lowly and reverently to all my betters' and 'to do my duty in that state of life, unto which it shall please God to call me'.

The Longer Catechism provides an interesting Scottish variant. Question ninety-nine asks: 'What rules are to be observed for the right understanding of the ten commandments?' Rule seven reads: 'That what is forbidden or commanded to ourselves, we are bound, according to our places, to endeavour that it may be avoided or performed by others, according to the duty of their places.' The emphasis is equally typical, perhaps, of the non-conformist strain in English church life and of the theocratic strain in presbyterianism. Secular authority must be kept under discipline and control. 'The squire and his relations' must behave themselves! The phrases 'according to our places' and 'according to their places' are significant. They underline the acceptance of a relatively stable social order within which each individual had a God-given place. Here is evidence of a stable tradition – which included, of course, religious beliefs and appropriate sex relationships.

Sex, society and 'the gods': these are the three areas within which adolescents must find appropriate modes of response. Who am I? How should I behave? What can I believe? These questions express the adolescent problem of ego-identity. When stable traditions begin to decay the typical patient of the psychiatrist needs support in his struggle to assert his real identity. When the tradition *has* decayed he needs help and support in the loneliness of human freedom and personal choice. Those who break down in the struggle may turn to the psychiatrist for assistance. Their contemporaries present teachers and parents with a difficult and delicate task.

Many of the distressing features of contemporary society have their source in the collapse of social support and direction. They are intensified by the anxieties of a nuclear age, by the intensity of the power struggle in national, international and interracial relationships, by the contrast between promise and performance in politics, by the complexity of contemporary life and the apparent impotence of the individual, by the magnifying influences of mass publicity. Neurotic forms of escape and neurotic forms of aggression are a natural human reaction. The adolescent problem of ego-identity becomes acute and pressing in such circumstances.

Erik Erikson has an appropriate comment on the deeper educational problems of social life. 'Each society and each age,' he writes, must find its appropriate 'form of reverence'. 'The clinician can only observe that many are proud to be without religion whose children cannot afford their being without it. On the other hand, there are many who seem to derive a vital faith from social action or scientific pursuit. And again, there are many who profess faith, yet in practice breathe mistrust both of life and of man.'² Each element in this quotation deserves separate consideration.

Each age must find its appropriate 'form of reverence'. This statement expresses the neutral standpoint of a clinical psychologist, but it provides support for a basic argument of this book. Men may be Christian or non-Christian, religious, agnostic or atheist, but all men are human. True human life begins in the awareness of death. Death symbolizes the mystery, and the menace, of conscious finite existence. At some stage – and especially, perhaps, in contemporary adolescence – we are all 'grazed' by the mystery of being and non-being. We may seek escape from it. We may rebel against it. We can only become mature, whole and free human beings by learning to live with our finitude. This task reaches the level of conscious response and decision in adolescence. It remains an uncompleted task throughout our mortal lives. Religious education should provide help in this task.

The second statement is equally important. : 'The clinician can only observe that many are proud to be without religion whose children cannot afford their being without it.' This is also a neutral statement. It claims that many children need the framework of religious belief and practice to support them in their personal development. It does not justify support for a full programme of Christian education in state schools. The argument against the possibility – or the desirability – of such a policy still stands. But it does focus attention on a fact which must affect our discussion of religious education at the adolescent stage. Secondary-school class rooms contain boys and girls at many stages of development towards personal maturity. They all need help but they need different kinds of help. The help they need most does not depend primarily on growth in religious knowledge or understanding at the intellectual level. The most important needs of adolescence, as of early childhood, lie below the level of consciousness. They are implicit, not explicit, religious needs.

All teachers play a part, consciously or unconsciously, in promoting the growth of their pupils towards personal maturity. This has always been a vital by-product of the educational process. We teach *John* as well as teaching John *Latin*. Nowadays the housemaster or housemistress is becoming the conscious focus of this educational task. Such members of a school staff fulfil a counselling function. They are members of the new secular priesthood which is emerging in modern society to meet the pressing problems of contemporary living. They play an important part in moral and religious education.

Such teacher-counsellors should be carefully selected and trained. The last two sentences in the quotation from Erikson are relevant at this point: '. . . there are many who seem to derive a vital faith from social action or social pursuits. And, again, there are many who profess faith, yet in practice breathe mistrust both of life and man.' Only the mature can help the immature to grow. It would be appropriate that teacher-counsellors should be selected from experienced men and women who have shown a special aptitude in human relationships. Some would be Christians but others might have no religious commitment. It would be desirable that they should all be given further training in modern techniques of counselling.

What would be the relationship between the functions of the teacher counsellor and those of the specialist in religious teaching? It should certainly be very close. They should both be members of a team of teachers prepared to accept responsibility for this aspect of school life. The leader of this team might be a specialist in religious teaching or a teacher with special training and experience in counselling. The responsibilities of the team would be partly pastoral and individual. They would also include participation in the type of group activity envisaged by Loukes's phrase 'dialogue in the class room'. Adolescent boys and girls need opportunities to talk freely together about matters of genuine adolescent concern – vocational problems, problems of personal relationships, current social and international problems, problems of meaning and purpose in human living, problems of personal belief. Such discussions must begin where the pupils are. They must be 'pupil-centred'.

This pupil-centred approach in religious education is constantly emphasized nowadays – and rightly so. All real education must have a focal point in the interests and needs of the growing mind and spirit. 'Dialogue in the class room' may often be therapeutic. It may help to release tensions and to promote growth. Yet the educational process needs two focal points – not one. Personal growth requires the guidance and stimulus of adult knowledge and adult tradition. If we neglect the pupil and his needs, knowledge may be acquired and pupils may pay lip service to adult traditions, but the knowledge will remain on the surface of their minds and the traditions will be forgotten in other environments. Their real thoughts and attitudes, their social values and their moral standards will develop under the pressure of inner needs and of social influences beyond the school frontiers. But there is an opposite danger. If we do not pay sufficient attention to adult knowledge and tradition 'dialogue in the class room' may become mere aimless chatter in which the blind lead the blind.

How far is it possible for humanists and Christians to co-operate effectively in moral and religious education during adolescent years? In October 1965, a pamphlet was published privately, but circulated widely, by a representative group of Christians and Humanists (*Religious and Moral Education: Some proposals for County Schools*, circulated by Howard Marratt, Borough Road College, Isleworth, Middlesex). Members of the group shared two common concerns. They advocated a more open approach in religious education and a more positive policy in moral education.

The pamphlet contained thoughtful and constructive proposals but it tended to cover over differences which need to be examined more deeply. One sentence illustrates this difficulty very clearly. The pamphlet states: 'It should be possible to agree on the principle of what is for Christians the second commandment: Thou shalt love thy neighbour as thyself.' Verbal agreement might be possible but practical interpretations would differ widely.

The principle of the 'second commandment' is not a very helpful guide in moral education. The word 'love' needs further qualification. Love of self takes many forms and concern for the neighbour can be expressed in diverse ways. The concept of love is certainly relevant to all aspects of human behaviour but the meaning of that concept is not easily defined. The second commandment, for the Christian, is inseparable from the first. The way in which love is expressed in action depends on the integrity and wholeness of Christian response to the first commandment: 'Thou shalt love the Lord thy God with all thy heart, and with all thy soul, and with all thy mind, and with all thy strength' (Mark 12.30 A.V.).

Can Christians and non-Christians move closer to each other at *this* point? Two quotations bring us to the heart of the matter. Erikson describes the final stage in the 'ripening' of 'basic trust' throughout the successive tasks and trials of the human life span as the stage of 'integrity'. In describing this stage he writes: 'We would expect trust to have developed into the most mature *faith* that an ageing person can muster in his cultural setting and historical period.'[3] John Macquarrie, describing the task of theology, writes: '. . . This discourse about God has to do with the most radical and concrete matters in life . . . where, exercising our freedom in finitude in all the light that we can get, we decide to take either the risk of faith, or the risk of unfaith.'[4] At this point the psychologist and the theologian, the neutral thinker and the Christian believer, seem to come very close.

'Is Being gracious?' We have met this question already. The Christian and the non-Christian part company in their answer to it but each answer involves risk. Christian and non-Christian alike confront the ultimate mystery of human existence and each goes forward in trust and acceptance, 'not knowing whither' he goes (cf. Heb. 11.8). Common humanity unites those whom religious belief may divide. Life can only be lived meaningfully by those who are continually aware of human finitude. The 'unexamined life cannot be lived'.

At this level of understanding it might be possible to secure verbal agreement even on 'the principle' of the first commandment. But such agreement, could it be reached, would be worth as little as agreement on the second. The real divergences arise at the lower levels of practical interpretation. Christians and non-Christians need to explore the meaning, and the implications, of both commandments for human living at all levels of understanding. Such exploration – extensive and prolonged – must precede any practical progress in devising a common plan for moral and religious education. Christians still want to begin with Christianity. Humanists still wish to avoid any semblance of religious commitment. Realistic analysis of the existing situation suggests a different type of 'open-ended' approach to the practical problems of moral and religious education.

The word 'love' is a useful signpost for such an approach. The word is widely used to describe an acceptable ideal for human living but the practical expression of that ideal in concrete situations arouses sharp disagreement. This fact is clearly illustrated in current controversy on sexual ethics, race relationships, the balancing of personal liberty against social welfare, the ethical problems arising from advances in scientific knowledge. Love and law may be in perfect harmony at the ideal level: at the practical level of human living they are in constant tension. The true claims of love are distorted by partial insights which have lost their relevance. Social prejudices and political passions cloud the real issues. In times such as these we cannot hope to solve the problems of moral and religious education by class-room dialogue arising from real life situations.

The pamphlet *Religious and Moral Education* seems to envisage county school pupils studying 'the Christian religion as part of their cultural heritage'.[5] It is indeed possible to undertake a study of this type. Such study may be open-ended in the sense that it leaves pupils free to accept or reject the Christian position but it may become an open-ended approach to a closed system of belief and practice. Few pupils have any strong urge to learn more about the Christian religion. Many of them have written it off as irrelevant. 'Open-ended' exposition of Christian teaching often implies a liberalized interpretation. This is likely to alienate pupils committed to a conservative position. It is not likely to inspire the uncommitted. It may throw little light on the issues which arise in class-room dialogue.

Authoritative teaching of 'revealed' truth is unacceptable. Adult direction of discussion is suspect. But uninformed debate is valueless. Can we penetrate behind the established and, for many contemporary adolescents, the fossilized forms of institutional Christianity and make an open approach to the original meaning of the word 'love' in the documents of the New Testament? Is it possible for

Christians and non-Christians to unite in a non-partisan study of the word *agape* in the thought and life of the primitive Christian church? Could such an approach be accepted as an appropriate element in the state-school curriculum of an age which pays lip service to the word but seldom penetrates to the depths of its original meaning? Real revolutions in human thought and action have often begun with rediscovery of the past. The tools are available for such a rediscovery in this field. Can Christians and non-Christians agree that an open-ended enterprise on these lines would provide the knowledge and insight needed to clarify and inform class-room dialogue on personal and social problems?

This suggestion has an important bearing on the selection and training of suitable staff and the preparation of appropriate text books. The material for study would be mainly biblical but the selection of material and the mode of approach would be different. The material would be drawn from the past but it should be presented and discussed in ways which expose its contemporary relevance. Teachers handling the material should have a level of specialized knowledge and professional training which would make their personal religious convictions relatively unimportant. Their personal convictions might be strong but their professional concern for tolerance and freedom of opinion should be stronger. Whether Christian or non-Christian they should share a common concern for the clarification of pupils' moral and religious perplexities. Teachers' beliefs should be subordinated to the professional task of deepening their pupils' insight and understanding and fostering their growth towards moral and spiritual maturity.

11 Towards a New Secondary Curriculum

A personal quest for 'new gods' is the characteristic task of adolescence. It is a peculiarly difficult task in modern society. The breakdown of the 'tribal mores' leaves the individual without social guidance and support as he faces the responsibilities and decisions of adult life. The task is never fully conscious and it is never wholly free. The primal balance of trust and mistrust still limits personal freedom. Mistrust and freedom are inversely related. The mistrustful individual is in bondage to inner fears and tensions. Who am I? What can I believe? How should I live? The modern adolescent's quest for an answer to these questions is often a blind, blundering struggle to escape from psychological bondage and to satisfy inner needs and aspirations.

The task of the school is obvious. Its responsibility for moral and religious education is urgent but its traditional tools are inadequate. School discipline may bring the horse to the water but it cannot compel him to drink. Modern adolescents distrust adult authority and many turn resentfully from the muddied waters set before them. They are conscious, at times, of thirst but the traditional waters do not satisfy them. They are troubled at times by doubts and perplexities but traditional answers seem unrelated to their questions.

Traditional teaching answers questions which adolescents have stopped asking. It seems unwilling to face the honest, searching questions which emerge from contemporary living. The concrete pointed questions of adolescence may arise from poignant personal experience and they are not satisfied by smooth abstractions. 'Why do parents batter babies?' 'Why do married people quarrel?' These spontaneous questions were asked by senior pupils of a large comprehensive school in an industrial area. Teachers may know that such questions demand knowledge and experience which the pupils do not possess. They may realize that, when pressed resolutely, they lead into deep waters of psychology, philosophy and theology. The wise teacher will try to enlarge their knowledge and deepen their experience and will lead them as far as they are prepared to go in deeper thinking. The Christian teacher may be convinced that the Christian doctrine of man offers the clearest guidance that he knows but impatient adolescents, like Pilate, will seldom stay for an answer at that level.

The demand for a 'life-centred' approach in moral and religious education arises from class-room experience and from class-room failure. This type of approach has an important place at all levels of age and ability. Roger Young's book, *Everybody's Business* (Oxford O.U.P., 1968), sets a standard, and suggests material appropriate for this approach in top forms of the secondary school. Harold Loukes's earlier book *Teenage Religion* (London: SCM Press, 1961) set out areas of adolescent concern within which fruitful learning might be fostered. His recent book, *New Ground in Christian Education* (London: SCM Press, 1965), contains two admirable chapters on 'Dialogue in the Classroom' which offer stimulating suggestions on syllabus and method. This approach is being exploited at many levels. Experience is accumulating and the limitations, as well as the possibilities, of the method are becoming clearer.

These limitations, and possibilities, are dependent ultimately on the quality and training of the staff. Reference has been made already to the contribution of 'teacher-counsellors' in class-room dialogue. The insight, experience and technique of a good counsellor have an important place in such dialogue at all ages. They are especially important in the younger forms and with inhibited or disturbed pupils. Dialogue in the class room should have a therapeutic function. It should promote emotional, as well as intellectual maturity. The latter is, indeed, intimately dependent on the former.

Adolescents do not reveal their deeper thoughts and feelings readily. They cannot articulate them easily but moments of genuine personal discussion may be sparked off unexpectedly in various ways. They may arise spontaneously from reaction to some current happening, to an extract from a newspaper, a TV documentary or a radio programme. The technique of role playing may be used to expose beliefs and attitudes not easily expressed. An imaginary situation may be described from family life, from the coffee bar, from the dance hall. Pupils will enter into the situation imaginatively by accepting a particular role in the incident. They may act it out or they may express their thoughts in writing. In either case a live discussion may be initiated. The teacher will naturally play a part in such discussion but he will speak as a member of the group and not as a final authority. As Loukes himself says: 'If our youngsters get the impression that there are certain "right" answers towards which they are being gently manipulated, if they feel that they are being "brainwashed", however painlessly, they will close up at once.'[1]

Moral and religious education in a state school should be controlled and directed by a team of teachers and counsellors with varied gifts and abilities. They should also represent different religious and non-religious traditions. In future years large secondary schools might include Roman Catholic as well as non-Roman Catholic pupils and the Roman Catholic Church might be included among the religious traditions represented. The allocation of time and the administrative details would vary in individual cases but two principles seem worth stressing. The 'life-centred' approach should determine one element in the curriculum from the age of thirteen years. There should be as much opportunity as possible for considering different viewpoints by interchange of teachers, by using visitors with special knowledge and experience, by hearing and discussing radio programmes, by joint class meetings using interview techniques and in other ways. This should enable pupils to hear different views presented with personal conviction and to submit them to critical scrutiny. The values of personal conviction may be conserved in this way without fear of adult indoctrination.

The second principle has already been stated. Its practical implications should now be examined. In a 'post-Christian' society it seems legitimate to claim a place for serious, and non-partisan examination of the origins and essence of Christian belief and life. The much used, and frequently abused word 'love' has a distinctive meaning in early Christian documents. Its relevance to problems of personal development, personal relationships and contemporary social and international problems is widely recognized. The word itself is likely to be used frequently in class-room dialogue. What does the word mean and what does the rule of love imply in human living? The word itself is central in Christian belief and practice but its meaning, in contemporary use, is constantly distorted by human failure and misunderstanding. Clarity in class-room dialogue requires fresh insight into the original Christian documents and deeper understanding of their perennial relevance to the human predicament. Such insight and understanding demands solid study and hard thinking from staff and pupils at levels appropriate to their several capacities. The semantic bridge between the concrete, and often poignant questions of pupils and the insights of early Christian belief and practice cannot be built quickly but a light-hearted attempt to leap across offers no lasting solution. An age which asks searching questions will not be satisfied with easy answers.

Study of the original meaning of *agape* in Christian documents should be focused on Christian teaching about the death and resurrection of Jesus. A distinctive pattern of belief and life emerged in eastern Europe at the beginning of the Christian era. The pattern has been distorted and broken but it has never wholly disappeared. This is a fact of human history. Christians, and many non-Christians in contemporary Europe, still regard 'the riddle of a life lived and a death died' as central for our understanding of the meaning of love in human relationships. Many non-Christians would also admit, surely, that any attempt to explore the mystery of human existence in schools which have inherited the Christian tradition should begin at this point. They would insist, and rightly so, that any study of Christian origins and of Christian insights should be open and unbiased. Knowledge and understanding should be our aim. Acceptance or rejection should be the fruit of mature personal decision.

The Bible is our main source book when we seek deeper insight into the source and nature of Christian love but it is a baffling book for modern adolescents. It spoke simply and directly in earlier days to those who had been brought up within a living Christian tradition. We live now in a different age. The archaic thought forms of the Bible present difficulties which no modern translation can overcome. The Bible is a difficult book today for those who have been brought up in Christian homes. It must often seem incomprehensible to those who have no inner clue to the meaning of religious language. Our main concern for all our pupils is that they should gain deepening insight into the Christian meaning of love. We are not training young theologians or biblical specialists. The most urgent task of the school is to educate for life – and for death. Our method must include study of biblical passages but a great deal of factual knowledge will be needed for meaningful interpretation of these passages.

In the earlier years of the secondary school this element in the curriculum must be adjusted to suit varying levels of academic ability. Two aims should be kept in view. The preparatory factual teaching of the primary school should be supplemented. Pupils should become familiar with the outstanding men and events of Israel's history. They should become familiar with the prophets' interpretation of that history in terms of vocation, failure and hope. They should learn more about the political, social and religious setting of Jesus' life and death. They should begin to recognize the contrast between the Messiah of popular Jewish expectation and the Messiah of Christian belief. The selection of appropriate biblical material should be governed by the ultimate intention of the course. Familiarity with narratives from the Old and New Testaments is less important than factual knowledge which may deepen understanding of Jesus's life and death. Biblical knowledge is not an end in itself.

The course for the first three years of the secondary school should also familiarize pupils with men and women of all ages and from many cultures who have lived lives of outstanding human worth. Pupils should know about Socrates and Gautama as well as about Amos and Jesus. The curriculum should have a practical outlet in appropriate activities expressing social concern. It might include studies of worship in different religious traditions. This could be a more fruitful introduction to comparative religion than fourth and fifth form courses on eastern beliefs. A fresh critical approach to the sources of their own heritage will be more rewarding than superficial study of beliefs which have their roots in a radically different culture.

The Hebrew prophets' interpretation of history offers one answer to the enigma of human existence. It is both an optimistic and a pessimistic answer. It is pessimistic in its frank acceptance of the harsh realities of nature and of history. It is optimistic in its hope for a transformation of nature and for the fulfilment of divine perfection within the troubled life of man. It stands in sharp contrast with the world-renouncing philosophies of Brahmanism, Buddhism and Graeco-oriental mysticism. It knows that man is fallible and frail but it looks for the fulfilment of man's true nature in obedience to the divine will. The messianic hope of the prophets looks for the ultimate triumph of good over evil through the mercy and judgment of God. The Christian claim 'Jesus is the Messiah' might be said to fulfil the deepest elements in that hope. It certainly involved rejection of contemporary Jewish attempts to find personal and social perfection.

The Pharisees, Essenes, Zealots and Sadducees provide instructive evidence of Jewish failure to reconcile perfect obedience to a divine law with the imperfections of fallible human nature. The Pharisees tried to lead a whole nation into paths of perfect obedience. The Essenes withdrew from the world in their search for perfection. The Zealots believed that evil political rulers must be resisted and overthrown in the service of God. The Sadducees used political power to safeguard religious traditions. None of these groups found an answer to the poignant contrast between the soaring hopes of the human heart and the failure of the human will, between human dreams of perfection and the harsh realities of human existence.

Christian teaching has its roots in the theme of divine grace which lies at the heart of Old Testament tradition. The prophets describe Israel's disobedience to the divine law as blind ingratitude. 'The ox knows its owner and the ass its master's crib; but Israel does not know, my people does not understand' (Isa. 1.3). The power of love to heal the divisions in human nature is foreshadowed in Old Testament scripture (cf. Jer. 31.31-34; Ezek. 34.11; 36.26; Isa. 53.5). It becomes the central theme of New Testament teaching. The New Testament writers claim that such healing begins when men acknowledge and respond to the 'supernatural' love manifest in Jesus's life and death (cf. II Cor. 5.14-17; I John 4.10; Eph. 2.8).

A syllabus for senior academic pupils studying Christians origins should begin in history with the emergence of the Christian movement within the Roman world. It should examine critically the claims which these Christians were making. Two facts would stand out at once. They were expressing their claims in the language of Jewish belief and hope. The Christians were claiming that these beliefs and hopes had been fulfilled in the life and death and, they said, in the resurrection of a crucified Jew. This fact would be obvious at once. Jewish scriptures were being reinterpreted by these Christian claims. Traditional Jewish hopes and beliefs were being transformed. This fact would soon become obvious. At this point it would be desirable to examine the earliest Christian writings – the early letters of the New Testament. These are the first documents of the Christian movement. They provide the earliest evidence for Christian belief and they show its roots in Old Testament tradition. A few illustrative examples should be studied.

Paul draws a parallel, for instance, between Jesus and Adam. He refers back to Gen. 2.7: 'Then the LORD God formed man of dust from the ground, and he breathed into his nostrils the breath of life; and man became a living being.' He writes 'The first man Adam became a living being' and he adds 'the last Adam became a life giving spirit' (I Cor. 15.45). This parallel takes us to the heart of Paul's teaching about the death and resurrection of Jesus but the parallel cannot be understood fully without a study of the myth of the Fall. That myth traces the tensions, discords and strife of personal and social life to primal distrust. Ego-centric fears and demands are rooted in the insecurity of the creature who distrusts his creator. Man's awareness of finitude rouses doubts and fears which no human effort can finally still. The human quest for personal freedom and enduring satisfaction derives its poignancy from that fact.

Paul and the writer to the Hebrews dwell on the significance of Abraham in Jewish tradition and in Christian faith. Abraham is not merely the traditional ancestor of the Hebrew race. Paul sees him as the father of all who live by faith. The story of Abraham and his sacrifice of Isaac takes on a new meaning. It becomes a foreshadowing of the commitment in trust and obedience which marks the Christian way of life. The writer to the Hebrews sees Abraham as one who 'went out' at the call of God 'not knowing where he was to go' (Heb. 11.8). He sees Jesus as the 'pioneer and perfecter' of this attitude of faith. Jesus's death on the cross becomes the symbol of Christian trust. Jesus, too, went out in trust and obedience 'not knowing whither he went'.

Moses is another key figure in Jewish scriptures and in Christian writings. 'For the law was given by Moses; grace and truth came through Jesus Christ,' wrote the fourth evangelist (John 1.17). The relationship between law and grace is a central theme in Paul's letters. Israel had tried to obey the law and had failed. The death of Jesus the Messiah had opened a new possibility in human living. The constraint of law had been superseded by the power of grace. The old distinction between Jew and Gentile had become meaningless. The followers of Jesus – whether Jews or Gentiles – were the true Israel of God. (Gal. 6.16). They had inherited the unfulfilled vocation of Israel and they were heirs of God's promises to Israel –

'heirs of God and fellow-heirs with Christ' (Rom. 8.17).

The Hebrew prophets looked forward to a day of personal and social renewal in human life: 'Then justice will dwell in the wilderness and righteousness abide in the fruitful field. And the effect of righteousness will be peace, and the result of righteousness, quietness and trust for ever' (Isa. 32.17). The New Testament writers claimed that that day had dawned. The death and resurrection of Jesus marked the beginning of God's rule among men. The power of evil had been broken and God's new age was beginning. The Second Isaiah's portrait of the suffering servant of God by whose stripes 'we are healed' played a prominent part in Christian thinking about the death and resurrection of Jesus. The second chapter of I Peter quotes freely from Isa. 53 in its description of Jesus. Jesus the Messiah had opened a way of renewal for human life by his suffering and death. The path to fuller life led through the gates of death. Ego-centric claims for temporal satisfaction must yield to a larger loyalty and a richer, though intangible hope. A life which conquers death begins in this world. The Christian dies with Christ and rises again 'in newness of life' (cf. Rom. 6.4). The larger Christian hope has its roots in that knowledge of God which 'is eternal life' (John 17.3).

The link between early Christian belief and Old Testament scriptures is obvious and inescapable. An objective and creative approach to Christian belief and life must interpret early Christian writings in the light of constant Old Testament references. This study can be carried out in various ways and at different levels. Some such study is essential for deeper insight into the meaning of *agape* as the first Christians understood it. It is a desirable introduction to the study of the Gospels at this stage of school life. The Gospels are not unbiased records of historical happenings. They are an extension and justification of Christian preaching. Study of Christian beliefs at their formative stage may help to overcome difficulties which arise in a critical approach to the Gospels.

Pupils who make this approach to the Gospels may be ready to understand the relationship between historical fact and Christian interpretation in the Gospel records. They will be ready to compare and contrast the ways in which the four Gospel writers have introduced their theme. They will recognize the true significance of the birth stories and the contribution which they make to Christian understanding of the person of Jesus. They will see that the prologue of the fourth Gospel fulfils the same function in another way. Luke begins with narratives of supernatural happenings at the time of Jesus's birth. John says: 'In the beginning was the Word . . . and the Word was made flesh and dwelt among us.' Both are preparing their readers for an account of the events associated with the life and death of the one whom they have come to recognize as the 'Son of God'. Pupils will recognize also the Christian angle from which John the Baptist is presented in the Gospels. John the Baptist figures in Jewish and in Christian history. Josephus, the Jewish historian, gives a Jewish account of him. The Gospels present him as the expected Elijah of Jewish tradition, the forerunner of the Messiah. History is interpreted in the light of Christian belief.

Senior pupils should be encouraged to read books like Hugh Schonfield's *The Passover Plot* (London: Hutchinson, 1965) and *Those Incredible Christians* (London: Hutchinson, 1967). They will know that such books exist. We should not attempt to hide the fact that the historical realities of Jesus's life are obscure and uncertain. Any such attempt would contradict our non-partisan intentions. It would not do justice to the diverging views of Christian scholars. It would be unfair to non-Christian colleagues and pupils.

When pupils study the miracle stories and read the resurrection narratives in the Gospels they will be ready to interpret the meaning of such passages. They will not stumble unnecessarily over the problem of historicity. Some may decide eventually that 'the bones of Jesus lie somewhere in Palestine'.[2] They will recognize, however, that such 'historical' (*historische*) scepticism does not dispose of the Church's claim: 'Christ is risen.' They will be ready to look beyond the narratives of an empty tomb to the new life which the first Christians shared with him whom they called their 'Risen Lord'. They may learn to see in it the inner meaning of the resurrection experience and the most convincing evidence for the early Christian's verbal claim.

When they reach that point of insight they may begin to understand the meaning of Christian faith and the depth of Christian love. They may recognize that Christian faith is not a superior kind of assured knowledge. They may see in it a venture of trust and commitment to the perfect love symbolized in the cross of Jesus. They may begin to understand that Christian love is not a norm of everyday living. It is a constant stimulus and a constant rebuke. Love may prompt us to reject traditional standards of social behaviour.

Law as well as love must guide us as we seek new and better standards to take their place. A 'new morality' must pay more attention to the healing power of love. It must also avoid the starry-eyed sentimentality which ignores the restraints of law and custom in personal and social living. The appropriate relationship between law and love in a 'fallen' world lies at the heart of many ethical problems which concern adolescents. Deeper insight into the 'riddle of a life lived and a death died' might help to clarify discussion of these problems.

The healing work of *agape* is not complete. The fulfilment of the Christian hope began within history but it looks beyond history (cf. Eph. 1.13f.). Non-partisan study of the origin and nature of *agape* must acknowledge frankly the tragic failures of Christian history. The path of perfect love, like authentic existence, is a standard of perfection which beckons but continually defeats the human will. Christian teaching differs from non-Christian existentialism in acknowledging the 'incarnation' of perfect love in Jesus the Messiah. It claims that response to that love, in trust and obedience, opens channels of healing power in personal and social living. Christian history from the first century to the present day can show evidence of that creative power at work in human nature and in human relationships. The dark side of Christian history must be acknowledged frankly but the other side must not be ignored.

The moral dilemmas of contemporary society cannot be resolved by using perfect love as a norm for everyday living. It is an impossible norm for the human will. Every generation since the beginning of Christian history has evolved rules in which the absolute norm has found temporary expression appropriate to the needs and limitations of the age. Throughout all Christian generations prophetic voices have been raised in protest against the denial of love's claims in this or that aspect of human life. These protests have been the fruit of prophetic insight. They have been evoked by Christian failure and by social changes which have created new problems in human living. Our own age is an extreme example of rapid change in social needs and in human attitudes. It calls for clear thinking, prophetic leadership and wise planning. Christian ethical guidance must always acknowledge the norm of perfect love. It must seek continually to interpret that absolute standard in ways appropriate to the needs and possibilities of the age in which we live. Study of *agape* in early Christian belief and life may throw fresh light on the moral confusion and perplexity of our times.

The appropriate aims and intentions of religious education in state schools might be summarized in words attributed to F. W. Sanderson, who was headmaster of Oundle School from 1872 to 1922: 'We must march boys up to the frontiers of the unknown.' 'The frontiers of the unknown' are the growing point of human knowledge, the limits of human achievement. It is at the frontiers of the unknown that we touch mystery, that man meets 'God'. 'No one has ever seen God,' wrote St John the evangelist. This is the unknown God, the unknowable God, of natural religion. If we can awaken our pupils to an awareness of the mystery we shall have *begun* to fulfil the appropriate purpose of religious education in a state school curriculum.

But St John had other words to say: 'The only Son, who is in the bosom of the Father, he has made him known.' We shall *fulfil* the aims appropriate to religious education in the state schools of today and tomorrow if we deepen our pupils' insight into the Christian symbols of the cross and the empty tomb. The cross symbolizes the depth of suffering which perfect love involves in a loveless world. The empty tomb points to the victory of such love over sin, suffering and the power of death. This is the Christian message of healing and renewal for human living. It is the Christian interpretation of the mystery at the frontiers of human existence.

Notes

Notes

Chapter 1

1 J. Wilson, *et al.*, *Introduction to Moral Education* (London: Penguin Books, 1967), p. 177.

2 E. Cox, *Changing Aims in Religious Education* (London: Routledge and Kegan Paul, 1966), p. 66.

3 *Ibid.*, pp. 66f.

4 *Ibid.*, p. 67.

5 J. Wilson, *Aims of Education in Religion and the Emotions* (1967), p. 3.

6 *Ibid.*, p. 4.

7 P. R. May, 'Why Parents Want Religion in School', *Learning for Living* (March 1967), p. 16.

8 E. Cox, *Sixth Form Religion* (London: SCM Press, 1967), pp. 16f., 120f.

9 J. A. T. Robinson, *Honest to God* (London: SCM Press, 1963), p. 8.

Chapter 2

1 Introductory Note to the Revised Edition of 1939.

2 Education Act, 1944, Sect. 26, para. 1.

3 H. Loukes, *Religious Education, 1944-84* (London: George Allen and Unwin, 1966), pp. 59f.

Chapter 3

1 B. Russell, *The Autobiography of Bertrand Russell: 1914-44* (London: George Allen and Unwin, 1968), p. 118.

2. L. Wittgenstein, *Tractatus Logico-Philosophicus* (London: Routledge and Kegan Paul, 1949, reissue), 6.52, 6.521.

3 *Ibid.*, 6.522.

4 L. Wittgenstein, *Philosophical Investigations*, 2nd ed. (Oxford: Basil Blackwell, 1967), p. 224e.

5 I. T. Ramsey, *Religious Language* (London: SCM Press, 1957), p. 11.

6 I. T. Ramsey, *Models and Mystery* (London: Oxford University Press, 1964), p. 2.

7 *Ibid.*, pp. 13f.

8 *Ibid.*, p. 28.

Chapter 4

1 Wilson, *et al.*, *Introduction to Moral Education*, p. 177.

2 *Ibid.*, p. 27.

3 *Ibid.*, pp. 113f., 116.

4 R. S. Peters, *Ethics and Education* (London: George Allen and Unwin, 1966), p. 15.

5 *Ibid.*

6 *Ibid.*, p. 232.

7 *Ibid.*

8 *Ibid.*

9 *Ibid.*, p. 234.

10 *Ibid.*, p. 114.

11 *Ibid.*, pp. 164ff.

12 *Ibid.*, p. 232.

13 D. Bonhoeffer, *Letters and Papers from Prison* (London: Fontana Books, 1959), p. 93.

14 *Ibid.*, p. 11.

15 Simone Weil, *Gravity and Grace* (London: Routledge and Kegan Paul, 1952), p. 51.

Chapter 5

1 B. Berenson, *Sunset and Twilight* (London: Hamish Hamilton, 1964), p. 422.

2 *Ibid.*, p. 237.

3 B. Russell, *The Autobiography of Bertrand Russell: 1872-1914* (London: George Allen and Unwin, 1967), pp 185f.

4 A. E. Housman, *Last Poems* (London: Grant Richards Ltd., 1922), p. 26.

5 M. Heidegger, *Being and Time* (Oxford: Basil Blackwell, 1967), p. 396.

6 M. Heidegger, *Existence and Being*. Selections with introduction by Werner Brock (London: Vision Press, 1949), pp. 287-291.

7 L. Wittgenstein, *Tractatus Logico-Philosophicus*, 6, 522.

8 *Ibid.*, 6.44.

9 J. Macquarrie, *Studies in Christian Existentialism* (London: SCM Press, 1966), p. 11.

10 A. Flew and A. MacIntyre, eds., *New Essays in Philosophical Theology* (London: SCM Press, 1955), pp. 184f.

Chapter 6

1 E. Jones, 'The Psychology of Religion', *British Journal of Psychology*, VI, 1926, p. 268.

2 S. Freud, *The Future of an Illusion* (London, Hogarth Press, 1927), p. 52.

3 *Ibid.*, p. 54.

4 E. Erikson, *Childhood and Society* (London: Penguin Books, 1965, first published in the U.S.A. in 1958), p. 74.

5 P. Tillich, *Systematic Theology*, II (London: Nisbet, 1957), p. 39.

6 Cf. Erikson, *Childhood and Society*, p. 201 note.

7 *Ibid.*, p. 242.

8 C. G. Jung, *Psychology and Religion* (London: O.U.P., 1938), p. 42.

9 R. Wilhelm and C. G. Jung, *The Secret of the Golden Flower* (London: Kegan Paul, Trench, Trubner & Co., 1938), pp. 123, 132.

10 C. G. Jung, *The Integration of the Personality* (London: Kegan Paul, Trench, Trubner & Co., 1940), p. 289.

11 Jung, *Psychology and Religion*, p. 47.

12 *Ibid.*, p. 99.

13 Erikson, *Childhood and Society*, p. 262.

14 *Ibid.*, p. 260.

15 *Ibid.*

16 *Ibid.*, p. 271.

Chapter 7

1 *The Christian Education of Youth* (London: Catholic Truth Society, 1949), p. 8.

2 *Ibid.*, p. 41.

3 R. Rees, 'A New Movement in Religious Education in China', *Religion in Education*, vol. I, no. 2 (April 1934), p. 79.

4 'An Open Letter to L.E.A. Advisory Committees' (circulated over the signatures of Ronald Goldman and others, 1965).

Chapter 8

1 J. Piaget, *The Child's Conception of the World* (London: Kegan Paul, 1929), p. 354.

2 W. McDougall, *Social Psychology*, 17th ed. (London: Methuen, 1922), p. 122.

3 Piaget, *The Child's Conception of the World*, p. 354.

4 *Ibid.*, p. 353.

5 P. Bovet, *The Child's Religion* (London: Dent, 1928), pp. 11, 39f.

6 *Ibid.*, p. 59.

7 R. Goldman, *Religious Thinking from Childhood to Adolescence* (London: Routledge and Kegan Paul, 1964), p. 2.

8 *Ibid.*, p. 3.

9 *Ibid.*, pp. 247-263.

10 R. Goldman, *Readiness for Religion* (London: Routledge and Kegan Paul, 1965), pp. 50-52.

11 J. Macmurray, *Search for Reality in Religion* (London: George Allen and Unwin, 1965), p. 17.

12 Bovet, *The Child's Religion*, pp. 126f.

13 M. Klein, *Our Adult World and Its Roots in Infancy*, Tavistock Pamphlet No. 2 (London: Tavistock Publications Ltd., 1960), p. 4.

14 John Bowlby, 'Security and Anxiety', *The Listener* (March 17, 1966), pp. 383ff.

15 A. Maurer, 'Maturation of Concepts of Death', *British Journal of Medical Psychology*, vol. 39, pt. 1 (March 1966), p. 36.

16 *Ibid.*, p. 35.

17 *Ibid.*, p. 36.

18 Macmurray, *Search for Reality in Religion*, p. 18.

19 Erikson, *Childhood and Society*, p. 33.

20 V. Madge, *Children in Search of Meaning* (London: SCM Press, 1965), pp. 15f.

21 Quoted by Maurer, *British Journal of Medical Psychology*, vol. 39, pt. 1 (March 1966), p. 36.

22 Madge, *Children in Search of Meaning*, p. 14.

23 Erikson, *Childhood and Society*, p. 261.

Chapter 9

1 S. Isaacs, *Social Development in Young Children* (London: Routledge, 1933), p. 307 note.

2 Piaget, *The Child's Conception of the World*, p. 278.

3 Cf. P. Tillich, *The Courage to Be* (London: Nisbet, 1952), pp. 176ff.

4 Goldman, *Readiness for Religion*, p. 114.

5 *Ibid.*

6 Margaret E. Hughes, 'The Importance of Bread', *Readiness for Religion Work Cards* (London: Rupert Hart-Davies Educational Publications, 1966).

7 Madge, *Children in Search of Meaning*, p. 96.

8 *Ibid.*, p. 95.

9 P. Tillich, *Theology of Culture* (New York: Oxford University Press, 1959), p. 157.

10 Goldman, *Readiness for Religion*, p. 65.

11 *Ibid.*, p. 69.

12 *Ibid.*, p. 140.

Chapter 10

1 Erikson, *Childhood and Society*, p. 271.

2 *Ibid.*, p. 243.

3 *Ibid.*, p. 265.

4 J. Macquarrie, *Studies in Christian Existentialism* (London: SCM Press, 1966), p. 16.

5 *Religious and Moral Education*, 1965, p. 2.

Chapter 11

1 H. Loukes, *New Ground in Christian Education* (London: SCM Press, 1965), p. 163.

2 R. Gregor Smith, *Secular Christianity* (London: Collins, 1966), p. 103

Index

Index